Noël Coward's
Long Island Sound

**A Comedy of Manners in
Two Acts and Seven Scenes**

*Text edited from
the original by*

Barry Day

SAMUEL FRENCH, INC.

45 West 25th Street   7623 Sunset Boulevard
NEW YORK 10010   HOLLYWOOD 90046
LONDON   TORONTO

Copyright © 2003 by Noël Coward Estate

ALL RIGHTS RESERVED

CAUTION: Professionals and amateurs are hereby warned that LONG ISLAND SOUND is subject to a royalty. It is fully protected under the copyright laws of the United States of America, the British Commonwealth, including Canada, and all other countries of the Copyright Union. All rights, including professional, amateur, motion pictures, recitation, lecturing, public reading, radio broadcasting, television, and the rights of translation into foreign languages are strictly reserved. In its present form the play is dedicated to the reading public only.

The amateur live stage performance rights to LONG ISLAND SOUND are controlled exclusively by Samuel French, Inc. and royalty arrangements and licenses must be secured well in advance of presentation. PLEASE NOTE that amateur royalty fees are set upon application in accordance with your producing circumstances. When applying for a royalty quotation and license please give us the number of performances intended, dates of production, your seating capacity and admission fee. Royalties are payable one week before the opening performance of the play to Samuel French, Inc., at 45 West 25th Street, New York, NY 10010; or at 7623 Sunset Blvd., Hollywood, CA 90046, or to Samuel French (Canada), Ltd., 100 Lombard Street, Lower Level, Toronto, Ontario, Canada M5C 1M3.

Royalty of the required amount must be paid whether the play is presented for charity or gain and whether or not admission is charged.

Stock royalty quoted on application to Samuel French, Inc.

For all rights other than those stipulated above, apply to Alan Brodie Representation Ltd., 211 Piccadilly, London, W1J 9HF ENGLAND; info@alanbrodie.com

Particular emphasis is laid on the question of amateur or professional readings, permission and terms for which must be secured in writing from Samuel French, Inc.

Copying from this book in whole or in part is strictly forbidden by law, and the right of performance is not transferable.

Whenever the play is produced the following notice must appear on all programs, printing and advertising for the play: "Produced by special arrangement with Samuel French, Inc."

Due authorship credit must be given on all programs, printing and advertising for the play.

ISBN 0 573 62861 0   Printed in U.S.A.   #13807

No one shall commit or authorize any act or omission by which the copyright of, or the right to copyright, this play may be impaired.

No one shall make any changes in this play for the purpose of production.

Publication of this play does not imply availability for performance. Both amateurs and professionals considering a production are *strongly* advised in their own interests to apply to Samuel French, Inc., for written permission before starting rehearsals, advertising, or booking a theatre.

No part of this book may be reproduced, stored in a retrieval system, or transmitted in any form, by any means, now known or yet to be invented, including mechanical, electronic, photocopying, recording, videotaping, or otherwise, without the prior written permission of the publisher.

IMPORTANT BILLING AND CREDIT REQUIREMENTS

All producers of LONG ISLAND SOUND *must* give credit to the Author of the Play in all programs distributed in connection with performances of the Play and in all instances in which the title of the Play appears for purposes of advertising, publicizing or otherwise exploiting the Play and/or a production. The name of the Author *must* appear on a separate line on which no other name appears, immediately above the title, and *must* appear in size of type not less than fifty percent the size of the title type.

Credits must appear as follows:

Noël Coward's (50%)

LONG ISLAND SOUND (100%)

In addition, until May 25, 2007, the following credit must appear in all programs distributed in connection with the play:

The world premiere production of this play was produced by TACT/The Actors Co Theatre, in New York on 13 May 2002.

Noël Coward's
Long Island Sound

Text edited from the original by
Barry Day

was given its world premiere on May 13th, 2002 by
TACT/The Actors Company Theatre
at the ATA Theatre, New York

CAST
(in the order of appearance)

Agnes	*Suzanna Geraghty*
Louise Steinhauser	*Cynthia Harris*
Evan Lorrimer	*Simon Jones*
Lester Gaige	*Scott Schafer*
Bonwit Steinhauser	*James Murtaugh*
Irene Marlow	*Delphi Harrington*
Luella Rosen	*Patricia Randell*
Dwight Macadoo	*Daren Kelly*
Sergei Kerinyenko	*Kyle Fabel*
Bright Eyes Murphy	*Barbara Marineau*
Hughes Hitchcock	*Brent Harris*
Delia Hitchcock	*Rebecca Wisocky*
Mary-Lou Brancati	*Darrie Lawrence*
Don Lucas	*Rob Breckenridge*
Carola Binney	*Julie Halston*
Bob Hockbridge	*Greg McFadden*
Gloria Hockbridge	*Margaret Nichols*
Mrs Grouper	*Patricia O'Connell*
Charlie Schofield	*Charles Tuthill*

Directed by *SCOTT ALAN EVANS*

Set by *Troy Hourie*   Lighting by *Mary Louise Geiger*
Costumes by *David Toser*   Sound Design by *Daryl Bornstein*
Music arranged by *Jonathan Falman*

Associate Producer   *David Ries*

LONG ISLAND SOUND: **THE GENESIS**

Noël Coward and parties were not exactly strangers to one another but there were two in particular that, fortunately, ruffled social feathers enough to cause him to commit them to paper. The song *I've Been to a Marvellous Party* was inspired by a party in the summer of 1937 or 1938. (He could never remember which.) It was a time when no self-respecting American socialite could afford not to be seen in France, but when hostess Elsa Maxwell invited Noël, Beatrice Lillie and opera singer Grace Moore to her beach bash, they were lulled into a sense of false security by being told that they should come as they were, because it would be 'just ourselves'....

> *It was in the fresh air*
> *And we went as we were*
> *And we stayed as we were*
> *Which was hell!*

What was even worse hell was that 'just ourselves' turned out to be 'about a hundred of us, all in the last stages of evening dress' and it was made abundantly clear that the three of them were supposed to sing for their champagne and *foie gras* suppers. Noël refused point blank, although he had some recollection of Bea Lillie being coerced into singing. Grace Moore, he recalled, also 'held firm' — although in the lyrics he tells a different story.

> *Poor Grace started singing at midnight*
> *And didn't stop singing till four.*

The song was by way of being his revenge on the predatory Miss Maxwell, though it's doubtful if it even grazed her epidermis. But this was as nothing to the party from hell he had walked into some months earlier in February 1937. He and Gertie Lawrence were playing in New York in the hit *Tonight at 8.30*. Three different roles every night, several of them involving singing and dancing, were taking their toll and so, when society hostess Cobina Wright — a Maxwell *doppelgänger* of the day, who had the added advantage of her own money — invited him for a quiet weekend in the Hamptons, he unthinkingly accepted. He should have been warned by the car ride out there, where he was accompanied by Clifton Webb, drinking brandy and wearing 'ear muffs and a camel's hair beret'.

'All in all the journey seemed longer than the one on the Trans-Siberian railway, though without the amusing frontier stations.' When they arrived, he found himself in the next room to Webb, who proceeded to snore 'in the exact rhythm of the 'Hallelujah Chorus'. The next day he awoke to see from his window 'a long caravan of Rolls Royces and Pierce-Arrows ... like a funeral *cortège* for some eminent gangster, except minus the flowers.' The 'Just Us' had arrived. What predictably happened over the next several hours he turned into a 1939 story called "What Mad Pursuit" and subsequently into the 1947 play *Long Island Sound* (originally *House Party*).

Since many of the protagonists were still alive at the time, their identity was necessarily blurred in the telling but — had the play been produced – contemporary audiences would undoubtedly have recognised Cobina Wright in Louise Steinhauser and others. Grace Moore, Carole Lombard, a contingent of film cowboys whose names were household words splashing about in the indoor pool ... not to mention several second generation publishers *en famille* and the governor's wife of a minor British colony, to name but a few "who shall be nameless."

A small distraction was the fact that, once again Grace Moore insisted on singing a large part of her repertoire from "Mi Chiamano Mimi" from *La Bohème,* "Depuis le Jour" from *Louise* and a great deal in between, while refreshing herself 'from the mouth of a bottle of blended whiskey during the pauses.' Lily Dache, the milliner, managed to lose a valuable earring, which turned up in Monty Woolley's beard. The ordeal ended with Noël retiring to bed only to find it occupied by Cobina's husband, who had found his own occupied by the overly-emotional Miss Moore. At which point Noël packed his bag, tiptoed out of the house and hitchhiked his way back to New York, emulating the 'escape from chaos' ending he had used in *Private Lives* and was to employ in several later plays. As with so many projects, the moment for *Long Island Sound* seemed to pass. Director George Cukor considered making a film of it, Hugh Martin talked of turning it into a musical, but nothing came of either project — and into the Coward bottom drawer it went for more than fifty years.

But now, looking as it with all the characters safely and permanently 'offstage,' it can be seen for what it is — a comedy of bad manners. Times have changed in so many ways but the hedonism of 'The Long Island Set' has proved curiously impervious to it all. They still hunt in packs, the booze still flows – though, to be fair, there's Pinot Grigio amongst the hard stuff – and still nobody seems to listen to anybody else. Everything old is new again? It never went away.

Editorial Note

'Editing' is too strong a word for handling a Coward text; modifying is perhaps better.

The original script called for a cast of 27 which, as much as anything else, is a reason why it was unlikely to have been performed as written. The TACT production cut that down to 19.

In the published text I have restored three of the characters that were cut on the principle that other directors are likely to have other priorities.

LEONIE CRANE and SHIRLEY BENEDICT are a lesbian couple who do little more than appear as a token lesbian couple but LADY KETTERING in my view acts as a useful British foil to the

American 'establishment' view of MRS GROUPER.

Before the premiere production I had already removed four party guests — OTIS MEER, the dress designer, and GEORGE TREMLETT do nothing more than ask for and consume drinks, while FREDDIE and LAURETTE GROUPER WENDELMAN are merely around to pay court to MRS GROUPER.

The only change of significance I have made concerns Louise's servants. In the original the drinks were served — virtually non-stop — by two coloured servants AESOP and HENRY and, while this was perfectly consistent with 1947 practice, it would strike an inappropriate note today. Consequently, I have replaced them with an English Jeeves-type butler. Louise Steinhauser would wish to make a social 'statement' and such a snobbish importation would do that for her. It also seemed to me that there could be the occasional covert interplay between the two expatriate Britons — EVAN and JENKINS — cast away on this most alien of shores. In the TACT production it was decided instead to use an Irish maid AGNES. In the great tradition of other Coward comedy maids (*Blithe Spirit, Hay Fever, Present Laughter*, etc.) this substitution worked perfectly well. However, I prefer to emulate CRESTWELL, the omniscient butler Noël used in *Relative Values*.

While the play is not a 'period piece' requiring specific costume clues, it *was* written in 1947 and there are numerous references to that immediate post-war period which are intrinsic to the story and to the cultural transatlantic gap which existed at the time ... and in many respects still does. It is not recommended that the piece should be 'brought up to date' with topical references substituted. In its essence it has never dated.

As for the songs IRENE sings, they should ideally be Coward's. I suggest three of the lesser-known songs that do not come from specific 'book' shows — "Never Again," " Most of Every Day" and "The Dream Is Over."

— BARRY DAY
2003

CHARACTERS
(in order of appearance)

JENKINS: English Butler
LOUISE STEINHAUSER
EVAN LORRIMER
LESTER GAIGE
BONWIT STEINHAUSER
IRENE MARLOW
LUELLA ROSEN
DWIGHT MACADOO
SERGEI KERINYENKO (SUKI)
BRIGHT EYES MURPHY
HUGHES HITCHCOCK
DELIA: his wife
MARY-LOU BRANCATI
LEONIE CRANE
SHIRLEY BENEDICT
DON LUCAS
CAROLA BINNEY
BOB HOCKBRIDGE
GLORIA: his wife
MRS GROUPER
LADY KETTERING
CHARLIE SCHOFIELD

SETTING

The action of the play takes place
in the Steinhauser's home on Long Island
on an unspecified date in 1947

ACT I

Scene 1 The guest room. 2.30 am Sunday morning
Scene 2 The living room. About noon

ACT II

Scene 1 The guest room. About 4.30 pm
Scene 2 The same. An hour later
Scene 3 The living room. An hour and a half later
Scene 4 The same. Three hours later
Scene 5 The guest room. About an hour later

ACT 1

Scene 1

(A guest room in MRS BONWIT STEINHAUSER's house on Long Island.

Time: About 2.30 am on a Sunday morning.

The room is comfortably and charmingly furnished. On the audience's left there is a fireplace. In front of this there is a chaise-longue and an armchair. Above it, in the back wall, is a door which opens into a small hallway. Opening off this hallway is the bathroom and another guest room. None of this do we need to see. Against this back wall are two beds which face the audience. Below this are two windows. The walls are painted a pale eau-de-nil green and the whole effect both of furnishing and decoration, is one of restfulness and peace.

When the curtain rises, JENKINS, a Jeeves-type butler is just finishing unpacking and is in the act of laying out a pair of pyjamas and a dressing-gown on the bed, when the door opens and LOUISE STEINHAUSER, EVAN LORRIMER and LESTER GAIGE come in.

LOUISE is a good looking woman in the middle fifties. She is in an evening dress, because she has driven out from New York after dining and going to a play. EVAN LORRIMER, an Englishman of about fifty is in a dinner jacket. He is a quiet, intellectual man; a writer of some distinction and, both in appearance and behaviour, a model of what an Englishman of letters should be.

His hair is greying slightly at the temples, he has a small, neat moustache and an urbane smile. Perhaps there is a certain dryness about him. Perhaps every now and then he might incline a trifle towards pomposity, but these defects, if true, could only be perceived by the hypocritical.

LESTER GAIGE is agreeably and unmistakably an actor. He is wearing suede shoes, thin silk socks, very pale grey flannel trousers of exquisite cut, a bois de rose sweater with a turtle neck and a tweed sports jacket of extravagant heartiness. His age is somewhere between the late thirties and the early forties. He is carrying a Scotch highball in each hand.)

LOUISE. Really, I feel terribly. I bring you down to rest and keep you up to all hours talking.

LESTER. *(Putting down the highballs on a table.)* I've brought us each a little nightcap.

EVAN. I've already had far more than my usual ration.

LESTER. Who cares! You can sleep forever tomorrow.

LOUISE. Jenkins. This is Mr Evan Lorrimer. You must look after him devotedly and see that he has complete and absolute rest.

EVAN. *(Smiling.)* Good evening, Jenkins.

JENKINS. Good evening, sir.

LOUISE. This is the quietest room in the house, but you have to share a bathroom with Lester. I could have given you one downstairs with a bath to yourself but it isn't nearly so shut away and you might be disturbed by Bonwit getting up early or the servants or something.

EVAN. It's a perfect room.

LOUISE. I know how English people loathe central heating, so I have told them to have a fire for you all the time you are here, but if you'll take my advice you'll have the heat on a little bit as well, because the weather really is freezing.

EVAN. How very sweet and thoughtful of you.

LESTER. Louise is the kindest woman in the world. I've never known her say a harsh word to anyone — even in anger! Of course she's raving mad but one can't have everything, can one?

LOUISE. Be quiet, rat boy. I won't have you prejudicing Mr Lorrimer against me.

EVAN. We agreed to Christian names at supper. Please call me Evan.

LESTER. All this and Evan too.

LOUISE. You're slipping, Lester. That was originally said by Dorothy Parker.

LESTER. *Everything* was originally said by Dorothy Parker.

LOUISE. You can have breakfast in here or on the sun porch or in the living room or wherever you like. I've got special English tea for you. Cynthia Cawthorne sends it to me regularly from London every month. She's been wonderful all through the war. *(To Jenkins.)* Is everything unpacked?

JENKINS. Yes ma'am.

LOUISE. Well, then, you'd better go to bed. Mr Lorrimer will ring when he wakes. *(To Evan.)* Or would you rather be called?

EVAN. No thank you — I'd rather sleep until I wake.

LOUISE. All right then, Jenkins — good night.

JENKINS. Good night, Madam. Good night, sir.

EVANS. Good night.

(JENKINS goes out.)

LESTER. Don't you just adore Jenkins? Louise won't admit it but she got him in an auction at Sotheby's. Or won him at canasta. I forget which.

LOUISE. You know perfectly well he came to me when Binky Fotheringay lost his all at baccarat.

LESTER. Binky lost his all long before baccarat, sweetie. Fire Island, the word has it.

LOUISE. Ignore him, Evan. All I know is — I shall probably never be able to live up to Jenkins. But that is a cross I shall have to bear. By the way, there are English cigarettes in that box, in case you don't like American ones. I'm afraid I caught Jenkins sneering at them earlier, so I suppose I'll have to change them.

LESTER. I'm now going to tear off everything in a big way so as to leave the bathroom clear for you.

(LESTER goes off to the bathroom.)

LOUISE. Lester's a darling — I've known him for more years than I care to remember. He's utterly genuine you know — you can trust him *absolutely*. Once he's your friend, he's your friend for life and that's that.

EVAN. I like him already. I thought he was very amusing on the stage, too — and even more so driving down in the car.

LOUISE. I knew you'd like him — that's why, apart from you, he's the only one I've invited for this weekend. God knows, I detest big house parties but I daren't have a soul when he comes because he insists on being quiet. He says he gives out so much at every performance during the week that he'll be damned if he'll give a social performance on Sundays.

EVAN. I see his point.

LOUISE. He won't bother you because he does nothing but sleep. *(LOUISE takes a cigarette, lights it, and sits it down on the chaise-lounge.)* I'm awfully touched that you came — really I am. I know perfectly well that you were snowed under with invitations. I feel honoured — I mean that most sincerely.

EVAN. Nonsense. It is I who am honoured — and also very grateful. The impact of New York *is* a little startling, particularly upon someone who has never been to America before.

LOUISE. *(With simpering sincerity.)* It's hell, my dear. Let's not mince matters — it's a living hell. It's the war that's done it, you know — I swear it was never like that before. The war has been responsible for so many dreadful changes.

EVAN. It certainly has.

LOUISE. In the old days people entertained, of course, and gave dinners and dances and cocktail parties, but it was all somehow different. I can't quite explain — I'm absolutely idiotic whenever I try to express what I really mean — but now — in these last few years — everything seems to have become so vulgar. So much grace seems to have gone out of life. There are no manners any more. I attach enormous importance to manners, don't you?

EVAN. Manners are the outward expression of expert interior decoration.

LOUISE. How wonderful to be able to put things like that. You sound just like Oscar Wilde.

EVAN. Really, Louise — you embarrass me.

LOUISE. I mean it — honestly I do. When you know me a little better you'll realise that I'm utterly sincere. You'll also realise, I'm afraid, that I'm a moron — a complete moron — everyone says so. But I have a kind heart — even Lester admits that and he's bitchy about *everybody*.

EVAN. You don't appear to me to be in the least moronic. You strike me — even on our admittedly short acquaintance — to have wisdom, vitality and friendliness. It's a rare combination.

LOUISE. *(With a wistful smile.)* It's dear of you to say that. *(After a slight pause.)* Life is awfully funny, isn't it?

EVAN. Not monotonously so.

LOUISE. Ah, don't laugh at me. I told you I was idiotic at expressing myself. I didn't mean funny at all, really. I meant strange — unexpected — exciting.

EVAN. Yes. It can be all those things.

LOUISE. When I met you the other day at that horrible party and we talked and I saw how strained and tired you were — I suddenly realised something.

EVAN. *(Gently.)* What?

LOUISE. How lonely it must be to be a celebrity. To be constantly sought after, lionised and made a fuss of —

EVAN. I'm not as celebrated as all that, you know.

LOUISE. You're the most famous English writer alive today.

Your books have been translated into hundreds of different languages. You are read and admired all over the civilised world.

EVAN. You're exaggerating terribly.

LOUISE. No, I'm not. I've always longed to meet you. I'm a shameless snob about meeting people who really *do* things — and then when I did — well — *(She smiles.)* — I had a surprise.

EVAN. That sounds alarming.

LOUISE. I don't know what I expected, really. It's foolish to have preconceived ideas about people. But what I didn't expect, having read your books with all their wit and irony and almost clinical observation — what I didn't expect was to find a perfectly simple human being — and a vulnerable one at that.

EVAN. Vulnerable?

LOUISE. Yes. For once I haven't used the wrong word. Vulnerable is exactly what you looked, standing there with all those people yelling at you. My heart went out to you and in that moment I realised that in a small, humble way I could be of help. That's why I took my courage in both hands and bullied you into coming here for the weekend. I know only too well what New York can do to sensitive people, particularly if they are not used to it. All those awful parties and the noise and those hideous buildings closing in on you.

EVAN. Come now — the buildings are not hideous. It's a spectacularly beautiful city.

LOUISE. Soulless, my dear — utterly soulless. It gave me the most appalling nervous breakdown once, so I know what I'm talking about. I got to the point when I knew that I couldn't stand it for another minute. That's why I made Bonwit buy this house. He was a saint about it, though I don't believe he ever really understood. But now he's just as crazy about the house as I am. He has to go in every day, poor darling. We have an apartment at The Pierre. But I really hardly ever use it unless I go in for a party or an opening night or something and even then I often drive down here afterwards, however late it is. I swear to you it has changed my whole life. *(She goes over to the window and draws back the curtain.)* Look!

EVAN. Beautiful.

LOUISE. Do you know what that is?

EVAN. No — apart from being a great deal of water.

LOUISE. *(Triumphantly.)* It's The Sound. Do you see those lights twinkling far away on the horizon?

EVAN. Yes.

LOUISE. That's Connecticut. The place where the Yankee came from that Mark Twain wrote the book about.

EVAN. Louise — that was a terrible sentence.

LOUISE. Listen to the silence.

EVAN. *(After a pause.)* I'm listening.

LOUISE. It's a clear night, so the fog horn isn't going. Personally I love it when it does. It's a mournful noise but somehow reassuring.

EVAN. *(Quoting.)* The sea is calm tonight. The tide is full, the moon lies fair upon the straits —

LOUISE. Wordsworth?

EVAN. No. Matthew Arnold.

LOUISE. I knew it was somebody. *(She sniffs.)* Isn't the air wonderful? You know I've grown to depend on this utterly. You'd think you were miles away from anywhere, wouldn't you? And yet we're only actually a little way from New York. There are no houses near us — we're completely isolated. I warn you — there isn't a thing to do except lie about and relax. Bonwit plays golf occasionally and tennis in the summer but I don't play anything — I find at my age — I shall be forty-four next month — imagine! *(She laughs disarmingly.)* — I never try to hide my age, it's so silly and, after all, what *does* it matter? Anyhow, as I was saying — at my age I find that all I want are my comforts, nice books, a few real friends, not just acquaintances, and good food. I'm afraid that is all I can offer you — peace and good food and sleep —

(LESTER comes in. He is wearing a vivid dressing-gown over pyjamas of alarming simplicity.)

LESTER. You've been talking about sleep for the last three hours, darling. What about letting us all get some!

LOUISE. We were just talking about you. Evan adores you already.

LESTER. Just keep right on the way you're going, honey boy. If I see any signs of your passion waning, I'll scream the place down. The bathroom's all yours including my 'Nulife' laxative tablets. I left them on the shelf. They're bright green and I'm here to tell you — miraculous! You'll never look back.

LOUISE. Lester takes anything anybody recommends — it's a marvel to me that he's alive.

LESTER. You recommended these to me yourself, darling, when we were staying out at the Hearst Ranch — which shall be nameless. Where's my drinkie?

LOUISE. On the table.

LESTER. *(To Evan.)* Have you finished yours?

EVAN. No — I still have some left.

LESTER. Let me go and freshen it up for you.

EVAN. *(Firmly.)* No really — this is quite enough.

LOUISE. Would you like a glass of milk?

EVAN. No, thank you — really not.

LOUISE. Well, I really will leave you now. Good night.

EVAN. Good night — and thank you so very much.

LOUISE. Now, don't keep him up gossiping any longer, Lester. Finish your highball and go to bed. He is here to *rest*. I shan't expect to hear a sound from either of you until practically lunchtime.

LESTER. Which shall be nameless.

(LESTER waves his hand. LOUISE goes out. LESTER helps himself to a cigarette.)

EVAN. A woman of charm and great understanding.

LESTER. *(Strolling to the window.)* Louise is a riot. It's clouding over — it was as clear as crystal a minute ago and now look at the damned thing. Do you mind if I close the curtains? Wide open spaces always make me sick at the stomach.

EVAN. By all means.

LESTER. Do you mind if I go on talking while you go to bed?

EVAN. *(Without enthusiasm.)* Not in the least. Do.

LESTER. You're sure you wouldn't like me to freshen up your drink? It wouldn't take a minute.

EVAN. Quite sure, thanks. I'm not used to drinking very much.

LESTER. *(Settling himself on the chaise-longue.)* It's difficult to get in England now, isn't it?

EVAN. What?

LESTER. Scotch.

EVAN. *(Uncommunicative.)* Yes, it is rather.

(During the ensuing scene EVAN undresses slowly and methodically.)

LESTER. I adore England and everything about it including Bobbie Moxon. Do you know Bobbie Moxon?

EVAN. No — I don't think I do.

LESTER. He's a rugged character with a passion for Jane Austen.

EVAN. That's certainly a point in his favour.

LESTER. He knows all her books by heart. *Pride and Prejudice, Mansfield Park, Emma* and *Jane Eyre* —

EVAN. That was Charlotte Bronte.

LESTER. He adores the Brontes, too. He once dragged me all the way to Yorkshire to see where they lived. It was fantastic. Imagine them all thrashing about in that sinister little parsonage!

EVAN. Which shall remain nameless.

LESTER. *(Going into gales of laughter.)* You're divine — you really are! And I thought you were going to be the kiss of death. I nearly strangled Louise when she told me you were coming.

EVAN. *(Slightly nettled.)* In heaven's name, why?

LESTER. Well, to begin with, writers always terrify me. I once saw Theodore Dreiser through glass! Then there was all that publicity when you arrived, about the Book of the Month and English literature and you going on a lecture tour and whirling through all the old women's clubs like a dose of salts.

EVAN. You seem to have laxatives on the brain.

LESTER. *(Laughing again.)* You're quite right. They do everything to me — but everything! If you know what I mean —

EVAN. I can't help feeling that you are rather exaggerating their scope.

LESTER. You don't know me, honey. Unless I'm clean as a whistle inside every day of my life, I'm a dead duck.

EVAN. I still don't quite understand why you thought I was going to be the kiss of death — as you so graphically put it.

LESTER. I thought you were going to be very old indeed, pompous as all hell and without a grain of humour anywhere, and then what happened?

EVAN. Well, what did happen?

LESTER. Don't you know? Jesus! It was love at first sight!

EVAN. *(Laughing.)* You really are too ridiculous.

LESTER. That's better, dear — relax and let your hair down.

EVAN. At all events, I think I'll go and brush it.

(By this time he has taken off everything but his underclothes. He picks up his dressing-gown and pyjamas from the bed and goes to the door.)

LESTER. Leave the bathroom door open — I can't bear to be left alone for a minute.

EVAN. *(As he goes.)* All right.

LESTER. Shall I open the window for you?

EVAN. *(Off.)* Yes, please.

(LESTER rises from the chaise-longue, finishes his drink, lights another cigarette and goes over to the window. He pulls back the curtains, opens the window, sniffs the air for a moment and then

closes the curtain again. He scrutinises the books on the bed table then he goes to the door.)

LESTER. Have you read *Nightmare Alley*?
EVAN. *(Off. Obviously brushing his teeth.)* What?
LESTER. Have you read *Nightmare Alley*?
EVAN. Mmm *(Off.)* No.
LESTER. You should — it's the end.
EVAN. *(Off.)* The end of what?
LESTER. Just the end.
EVAN. *(Reappearing in pyjamas and dressing-gown.)* What are you talking about?
LESTER. *Nightmare Alley*.
EVAN. What's that?
LESTER. A book, honey — it's terrible — all about sex and circuses.
EVAN. I don't care for either.
LESTER. You should read it all the same. It's a radiant picture of American life.
EVAN. *(Going to the window.)* That smells good, doesn't it?
LESTER. I think people who live in cities are raving mad, don't you?
EVAN. Not always.
LESTER. I must say Louise has been a different person since she's had this house.
EVAN. Yes — she told me she'd had a bad breakdown.
LESTER. That was Hughsie.
EVAN. *(Puzzled.)* What?
LESTER. Hughes Hitchcock. She was crazy about him. They had a 'thing' for years and then he suddenly upped and married Delia. She was a Birdsall, you know.
EVAN. What on earth's that?
LESTER. A family. dear — don't get confused. A very famous Bostonian family. They all come from the North Shore and look it.

EVAN. Was all this before Louise married?

LESTER. Good God, no. She's been married for nearly thirty years.

EVAN. She must have married very young if she's only forty-four now.

LESTER. If Louise is forty-four now, I'm the late Mrs Stotesbury and something tells me I'm not.

EVAN. *(Dryly.)* I see.

LESTER. I've known her myself, man and boy, for the last twenty-five years. Man and boy is the operative phrase. I knew her when she first burst on New York — long before she met Bonwit. She was married to Ed Tinklor then. She was always an angel but her hats were misguided. They still are sometimes.

EVAN. *(With reproof in his tone.)* She's devoted to you. She looks upon you as one of the few people she can really trust.

LESTER. I'm devoted to her too. There isn't anything I wouldn't do for Louise. She's absolutely genuine, you know — once she's your friend she'll never change.

EVAN. *(Stiffly.)* I'm delighted to hear it.

LESTER. *(Sublimely unaware of disapproval.)* I was with her all though the Hughsie affair. It was amazing — it really was — amazing. She was nuts about him. She met him out on Grace Burton's ranch in Arizona. He was only a cowboy then, galloping about on a horse all day in 'chaps' and rounding up all those God-damned steers — which shall be nameless — and then she gave her all — if you know what I mean, and brought him to New York lock, stock and — what have you!

EVAN. *(Interested in spite of himself.)* What did Bonwit do about it?

LESTER. Nothing. He was in Europe at the time putting through one of those fabulous deals and when he came back it was all over and she was jittering about and taking overdoses and saying the skyscrapers were shutting in her soul.

EVAN. Has she ever seen him since?

LESTER. Oh yes — he and Delia live only a couple of miles away. It's all perfectly friendly.

EVAN. That must be a great relief for all concerned! *(He looks ostentatiously at his watch.)* Good heavens! It's after three! We really must go to bed!

LESTER. Have you got any of those things to stick in your ears?

EVAN. No.

LESTER. You must be out of your mind — they're magical. I'll get you some.

EVAN. No, really — I'm sure they won't be necessary.

LESTER. You never know what might happen. Bonwit might go trumpeting up and down the drive at cock-crow — you must have some — they'll save your reason. I won't be a minute. *(LESTER runs out of the room. EVAN takes off his dressing-gown and gets into bed. LESTER comes back with a little box.)* Here they are — have them by you just in case.

EVAN. You're very kind.

LESTER. Nonsense, honey — you're here for a rest and I would shoot myself if you didn't get it. If the slightest thing disturbs you, just pop them into your ears and you won't hear a sound. Shall I turn out the lights?

EVAN. Yes, please.

LESTER. *(At the door.)* Good night, sweetheart.

EVAN. Good night — honey.

LESTER. *(Going into gales of laughter again.)* Your sense of humour slays me — you're my pin-up boy for all time.

(LESTER switches off the lights, leaving only EVAN's bed light on, and goes out, closing the door behind him and still laughing.)

EVAN sits up in bed, frowning thoughtfully for a moment or two then, dismissing whatever doubts may be troubling him, he stretches luxuriously, yawns and puts out the light.

There is silence for a moment or two. Suddenly a fog-horn sounds close by. It is a depressing noise. A moment or two later it sounds again.

EVAN switches on the light, opens the little box that LESTER has left, takes two little wax pellets from it and rams them irritably into his ears. He switches off the light again.

The fog-horn moans once more as the curtain falls.)

Scene 2

(The living room.

Time: about noon on Sunday.

It is a large, light, impeccably furnished room. On the left is the door to the bar. Ideally the bar can be segregated from the rest of the room by sliding doors. These are usually kept open.

Close by is a card table. At the back of the set is a wide alcove leading to the hall, the stairs and the servants' quarters.

On the right, exactly facing the bar, is the French window leading to the sun porch. Downstage, below the sun porch is a large open fireplace around which are grouped several armchairs and a large sofa.

When the curtain rises, LESTER and EVAN, in pyjamas and dressing-gowns, are finishing their breakfasts at a small table just below the windows.)

LESTER. ... But you don't have to do a thing — you just lie there.

EVAN. I still don't think I should care for it.

LESTER. You relax completely and just say whatever comes into your mind and he sits right behind you. It's the most wonderful *release.*

EVAN. I loathe people sitting right behind me — it gives me the creeps.

LESTER. That's because you're all twisted up inside.

EVAN. I assure you I'm nothing of the sort.

LESTER. But how do you *know* you're not?

EVAN. Well, I eat and sleep normally, drink and smoke in moderation, work reasonably hard. I'm not tortured by any personal problems.

LESTER. What about your sex life?

EVAN. Unspectacular — and on the whole satisfactory.

LESTER. For all you know you might be seething with the most fantastic inhibitions.

EVAN. *(Equably.)* I might indeed.

LESTER. If you went to Dr. Gottlieb, he'd get them out of you in a flash.

EVAN. I don't want to go to Dr. Gottlieb and have all my inhibitions out in a flash. It might be most inconvenient.

LESTER. You must be *out* of your mind. He's magical! After all no-one can really *know* about their subconscious — consciously — can they?

EVAN. Why should they?

LESTER. Now listen, honey boy — you're just being obstructive — that's what you're being — and stubborn as an old mule. I'm here to tell you that you're missing the most wonderful *experience*! Dr. Gottlieb is fabulous. Look what he did for me!

EVAN. I don't know what you were like before.

LESTER. My dear, I was in the most terrible shape — practically mental. I couldn't eat or sleep, I cried incessantly from morning till night.

EVAN. Why?

LESTER. Well, you know — I was in love at the time — dear old l'Amour — which shall be nameless — and it was just after Pearl Harbour and I was playing in *And So What?* in Philadelphia.

EVAN. *And So What?*

LESTER. It never came into New York, thank God. If it had I should have been off the Empire State Building before you could say Brooks Atkinson.

EVAN. Who's he?

LESTER. *(Enraptured.)* Don't move! Stay as sweet as you are! Don't let a thing *ever* change you!

EVAN. What are you talking about?

LESTER. He's a famous critic, dear — who shall be nameless!

EVAN. If you say 'who shall be nameless' once more, I shall throttle you with my bare hands.

LESTER. It's merely a habit, dear, don't let it upset you. I catch a phrase every year like 'flu. Last season it was 'Yo-ho-ho and a bottle of scent'!

EVAN. Oughtn't we to go and dress? It will be lunch time soon.

LESTER. There you are, you see. I was perfectly right. You're a bundle of nerves and can't sit still for a minute. If only you'd take my advice and just *try* Dr. Gottlieb.

(At this moment BONWIT STEINHAUSER comes in from the hall. He is a large, red-faced man in the middle fifties. He is an amiable creature and is wearing plus fours.)

BONWIT. Hello, fellars.

LESTER. *(Jumping to his feet.)* Bonny — you look wonderful! This is Evan Lorrimer — Louise and I brought him down last night. He's crazy about the house and slept like a top.

EVAN. *(Rising.)* How do you do?

BONWIT. *(Motioning him down again.)* Don't move, for God's sake — it's good to see you — welcome to America.

EVAN. Thanks very much

BONWIT. Are they looking after you alright? Have you had enough breakfast?

EVAN. Quite enough, thanks — it was delicious. I apologise for not being dressed — I —

BONWIT. Stick around all day like that if you want. Nobody's formal here.

LESTER. Evan's here to relax — life was fencing him in and so Louise rescued him.

BONWIT. Good for her. How is she?

EVAN. She seemed very well last night.

BONWIT. I haven't seen her since Tuesday. Make yourselves comfortable. I'll be seeing you.

(BONWIT goes out again.)

LESTER. *(In an intense whisper — leaning across the table.)* You know, I *like* Bonwit.

EVAN. He seems very agreeable.

LESTER. I've *always* liked him.

EVAN. Is there any reason why you shouldn't have?

LESTER. He's a famous bore. We never dare to play the 'Tower' game when he's anywhere around — he gets thrown off over and over again — it makes one quite dizzy.

EVAN. I don't know the 'Tower' game.

LESTER. My dear, what do you *do* in England in the long winter evenings?

EVAN. Freeze.

LESTER. The 'tower' game is who you'd rather be left alone on a tower with if you had to – if you know what I mean.

EVAN. It sounds fascinating.

LESTER. It's guaranteed to cause the maximum row in the minimum space of time. My God, I'm witty as hell this morning. Are you impressed?

EVAN. You slay me.

LESTER. *(Laughing gaily.)* That's what I adore — when you're dry like that — it's heaven. We call it 'dead pan' over here.

EVAN. Thanks — I'll try to remember.

LESTER. Well — to get back to Bonwit.

EVAN. *(Resigned.)* If we must — we must.

LESTER. There's something awfully kind about him really *au fond* — French for 'at bottom', dear.

EVAN. Thank you.

LESTER. I have so leetle English – I amaze myself. Where was I?

EVAN. At bottom.

LESTER. Jesus — you're divine.

EVAN. I'm so glad.

LESTER. Bonwit's only really lethal when you get him on the subject of women.

EVAN. Why — doesn't he care for them?

LESTER. Care for them! My dear, he's crazy about them. Only they have to be blonde and they have to be dumb. You can always tell when he's in the grip of some brassy Diamond horseshoe number because he gets a roguish, butter-and-egg, club-car glint in his eye. That's the time to run. I must say he looked fairly tranquil this morning.

EVAN. What does Louise say to all this?

LESTER. Oh, she doesn't give a damn. She has her fun and he has his. After all, you're only middle-aged once.

EVAN. *(Curiously.)* Does Louise have much 'fun', as you call it?

LESTER. Not nearly enough — that's what's wrong with her — that's what's wrong with most of them. They get to a certain time of *La Vie* and expect life to be one long extravaganza. Then — if it isn't — they get bitchy as hell and then where are you?

EVAN. I suspect — exactly where you were before.

LESTER. Louise is all right up to date but I'm worried about her. That's why I made her go to Doctor Gottlieb.

EVAN. Has anything come of it?

LESTER. It's too early to tell yet. She's only had five treatments.

EVAN. Poor Louise.

(Sound of a car coming up the drive.)

LESTER. *(Springing to his feet.)* My God!

EVAN. *(Startled.)* What's the matter?

LESTER. *(At the window.)* It's all right — it's only Irene and Suki and Dwight and Luella. I though for a minute it might be strangers.

EVAN. *(Apprehensively.)* Are they coming for lunch?

LESTER. I expect so. You'll love Irene, she's divine — but *divine*! You've heard her sing, haven't you?

EVAN. No — I'm afraid I haven't

LESTER. *(Horrified.)* You've never heard Irene Marlow sing! You haven't lived, that's all — you just haven't lived. We'll make her sing after lunch — Suki's with her fortunately — he always plays for her. It's a lovely voice, one of those deep husky numbers. And there's somebody with an amazing sense of humour! You should see her when she's in a real rage with Dwight — Dwight Macadoo — that's her friend — to coin a phrase — my God it's terrific! Bang goes Sutton Place and out pops Iowa.

EVAN. Surely we'd better go and dress — I don't feel equal to meeting a famous Iowan singer in my pyjamas.

LESTER. You go, honey — and you might turn on a bath for me when you've finished. I'll deal with the visiting firemen.

EVAN. *(Going hurriedly.)* All right.

LESTER. *(Shouting after him.)* Slip into something loose, dear!

(There is the sound of voices in the hall.

After a moment IRENE MARLOW, LUELLA ROSEN, DWIGHT MACADOO and SERGEI KARINYEMKO (SUKI) come into the room.

IRENE is a fine looking woman in the early thirties. She has wide eyes and a generous mouth. Her voice is deep and attractive.

LUELLA is small and 'chic.' Her tailor-made outfit is perfectly cut. She looks exactly what she is, which is a buyer for a famous fashion magazine.

DWIGHT MACADOO is tall and handsome in a loose-limbed way. He looks as if he plays games a lot — which he does.

SUKI is a Russian who might be any age. He has a pale face and rather consciously wild hair.

LESTER embraces them all indiscriminately. They all drift into the room talking.)

LESTER. Irene, you look marvellous — Luella — how was Europe? — you must tell me *everything*. Hallo Dwight, you big gorgeous thing. Suki, you look as though you were going to be sick.

LUELLA. Suki always looks as though he were going to be sick.

SUKI. I have hangover.

LESTER. *(Practically.)* One Benzedrine and two aspirin. It's miraculous.

IRENE. He's already had three Benzedrine and eight aspirin.

LUELLA. I should think Dwight's driving would cure any hangover — I've never been so scared in my life.

DWIGHT. *(Amiably.)* I got you here, didn't I?

IRENE. We forgot the chains and had to go back to the garage for them. It's been a nightmare and I'm freezing.

(IRENE sits down by the fire.)

LUELLA. *(To LESTER.)* Scream for drinks, there's a darling. You're *Jeune Fille de la Maison*.

LESTER. Here's Jenkins now — he thinks of everything.

(JENKINS comes in and waits, with eyebrows raised, for their orders. So commanding is his presence that they cease their chatter until the business has been duly completed.)

LUELLA. Dream me up a nice 'old fashioned' will you, Jenkins?
JENKINS. Certainly, Mrs Rosen.

IRENE. The same for me. No Angostura, though. Thank you, Jenkins.

JENKINS. My pleasure, Madam.

LESTER. Dwight?

DWIGHT. Scotch highball, please.

LESTER. Suki?

SUKI. Tomato juice.

LESTER. Fatal — better have some gin in it.

SUKI. No — tomato juice good with vodka but not with gin.

LESTER. May we leave the matter in your capable hands, Jenkins? The whole thing is too '*ennuieux,*' as we say in Flatbush.

JENKINS. Indeed, sir.

(JENKINS leaves.)

LUELLA. *(To SUKI.)* We all know you're Russian, dear — you don't have to go bawling for vodka everywhere you go.

LESTER. Shall we all go into the bar?

IRENE. Not until life becomes insupportable out here — that bar gives me claustrophobia.

LUELLA. It's a good little bar as bars go, but it doesn't go far enough.

IRENE. It went quite far enough last time we were here — remember?

LESTER. That was the evening when Piggie and Chuck came to blows over the New Deal.

LUELLA. That's the first time I've ever heard poor Sylvia described as a New Deal.

(Everybody laughs at this.)

IRENE. Where's this British '*numero*' we've all been asked to meet?

LESTER. Flinging himself into some tweeds — you'll adore him.

IRENE. Give me three reasons.

LESTER. Well, he's a bit boxy, if you know what I mean.

IRENE. Quite frankly — I don't.

LESTER. Well — sort of remote, you know — shut up like a box.

IRENE. That sounds dreamy — I can't wait.

LESTER. But if you draw him out a bit he's sheer heaven.

LUELLA. In what way? Come on, darling — give — for God's sake — we're all on tenterhooks.

LESTER. Well he's quiet and quite witty at moments — dry, you know.

IRENE. Well, I suppose that's better than being wet.

LESTER. I can see that Irene's got a thing against him before she's even seen him.

LUELLA. She's been anti-British for the last six months — it's only because she takes *The Post* instead of *The Sun*.

LESTER. Well, he's a brilliant writer — you can't get away from that.

IRENE. I intend to get away from it as fast as ever I can.

DWIGHT. What's the guy written?

LUELLA. His last book — *A London Lady* — was a best seller. It was about the English Restoration — you know — Charles the Second. It was quite good.

IRENE. Like *Forever Amber*.

LUELLA. No — I will say that for it — it was *not* like *Forever Amber*.

IRENE. What does he look like?

LESTER. Absolutely awful — short and fat with little pudgy hands and as bald as a coot.

IRENE. Oh God — I knew it.

(JENKINS comes in with the drinks on a tray. Everyone helps himself and he leaves again.)

DWIGHT. I must say one thing for Louise — she's quick — she

manages to grab them practically before they've left quarantine.

LUELLA. That reminds me — where *is* our local Madame de Staël.

LESTER. She'll be down soon. We sat up for hours last night talking.

IRENE. No particular topic or just who's sleeping with who?

LESTER. Irene certainly got out of bed the wrong side this morning and if only we weren't all so certain whose — it might be more interesting.

(At this moment 'BRIGHT EYES' MURPHY comes in from the hall. She is a pleasant, easy-going woman, rather casually dressed.)

BRIGHT. Hallo, folks.

LESTER. *(Embracing her.)* Bright Eyes! How wonderful! Where have you come from?

BRIGHT. The Schaefers — Charlie loaned me his car. Hallo, Irene.

IRENE. Hallo, darling.

BRIGHT. Luella — I missed you by five minutes the other day at Pauli's. How was your trip?

LUELLA. Satisfactory on the whole.

BRIGHT. Is that hat part of it?

LUELLA. Yes.

BRIGHT. It's the best looking hat I've ever seen. Hallo, Suki. What in the world are you drinking?

SUKI. Vodka and tomato juice — I have hangover.

LUELLA. They're called 'Bloody Mary's. How *are* you sweetheart?

BRIGHT. Where's Bonny?

LESTER. He's about somewhere. He came breezing in while we were having breakfast, looking very red and healthy.

BRIGHT. He took the hide off me at Bézique last night. I've come to get my own back.

LESTER. *(Calling.)* Jenkins, will you inform Mr Steinhauser Mrs Murphy's here?

(BRIGHT EYES calls out.)

BRIGHT. Oh, and could I have a Coca-Cola, please, Jenkins? A little lemon and a great deal of ice.
JENKINS. *(Off.)* Certainly, Madam.
BRIGHT. *(Turning.)* Well — what's new — apart from Luella's hat?
LUELLA. Nothing much.
BRIGHT. How's the English novelist?
IRENE. Short and fat, with little pudgy hands and bald as a coot.
BRIGHT. Well, that'll be a change after Aldous Huxley.
LESTER. He's a riot — in a quiet way. You'll worship him.
BRIGHT. I'm sure I shall. What's he here for, anyway?
LESTER. One of those lecture tours — English literature of the Nineteenth Century. He's crazy about Jane Austen.
IRENE. Aren't we all?
BRIGHT. He doesn't do quaint Welsh folk songs at the piano, does he like Louise's last little surprise?
LESTER. I don't think so —but you never know — the British are terribly unpredictable.

(JENKINS enters with BRIGHT EYES' drink. She takes it. He exits.)

LESTER. Don't you want some gin with that?
BRIGHT. No liquor before sundown. It's a rule I learnt in the tropics.
IRENE. Which tropics?
BRIGHT. Palm Beach.

(BONWIT comes in from the hall. JENKINS follows him in and goes straight to the bar.)

LONG ISLAND SOUND

BONWIT. Hello, fellars.
LUELLA. *(Kissing him.)* Nobody can look as healthy as you do, Bonny — it isn't decent.
IRENE. Hallo, darling — forgive me for staying exactly where I am.
DWIGHT. *(Shaking hands.)* Where's Louise?
BONWIT. Stick around and you're bound to see her. Hallo, Suki.
SUKI. *(Gloomily.)* Hallo.
BONWIT. Come on, Bright Eyes — no sense in wasting time.
BRIGHT. That's my dream boy.

(They go over to the card table.)

IRENE. Oh, my God!
LUELLA. They're off.
BONWIT. What's the score?
BRIGHT. Don't pretend you don't remember.
BONWIT. You owe me forty-eight dollars.
BRIGHT. Forty-three, love — I got five back in the last game.
BONWIT. Okay.
BRIGHT. *(At the table.)* Cut for deal.
BONWIT. *(Cutting.)* Seven.
BRIGHT. *(Turning up a card.)* All right — go ahead.

(They settle down to concentrated Eight Pack Bézique.)

DWIGHT. Anybody feel like a game of backgammon?
IRENE. I'd rather die.
DWIGHT. Luella?
LUELLA. All right — three games.
DWIGHT. Come on then.

(DWIGHT and LUELLA settle themselves at a backgammon table just

above the sofa.)

IRENE. Why do people play games, Lester? Explain to me in a few brief phrases — why, when the god-damned world is filled with music and romance and atomic energy, must people play games?

LESTER. You're certainly in terrible shape this morning, darling — what you need is another little drinkie.

IRENE. Are you going to stay in that hysterical looking dressing-gown all day?

LESTER. I'll change when Sweetie Pie has finished with the bathroom. *(Calling.)* Jenkins — another 'old fashioned' for Miss Marlow and the same for me.

JENKINS. Very well, Mr Gaige.

LUELLA. *(Throwing dice.)* I hate that throw — I'll double it.

DWIGHT. Go right ahead.

LUELLA. *(Throwing again.)* Sweet God, that's worse!

BRIGHT. *(Laconically.)* Saying a hundred.

BONWIT. Eighty

BRIGHT. Saying a hundred.

BONWIT. Another eighty.

BRIGHT. Where did you get all those small trumps from?

BONWIT. Up my sleeve.

BRIGHT. At last — a hundred said.

IRENE. That's a hell of a relief to me.

(Sound of voices in the hall.
HUGHES HITCHCOCK and DELIA HITCHCOCK come in followed by MARY LOU BRANCATI.
HUGHES HITCHCOCK (Hughsie) is a tall, handsome man in the forties. DELIA (his wife) is about ten years younger; small and dark and quite attractive in a sharp pointed way.
The COUNTESS BRANCATI (Mary-Lou) is large and rather untidy. She also is in the forties and has pinkish hair and too much jewellery.

LESTER bounds to meet them.)

LESTER. Hughsie — Delia — Mary-Lou – this is wonderful — stomach in — it's only me.

MARY-LOU. Where is everybody?

IRENE. The dregs are here, dear.

MARY-LOU. *(Looking at SUKI who is sitting in an arm-chair gazing into space.)* What's the matter with Suki?

LESTER. *(Happily.)* Hangover — he looks frightening, doesn't he?

DELIA. Hello, Bonny. *(BONWIT makes a belated effort to rise.)* No — don't get up — Bright Eyes would kill me if I interrupted.

BRIGHT. Hallo, Delia — how are the children? Saying two fifty.

DELIA. Fine — they're over with the Caldicotts — Sunday's a day of rest.

HUGHSIE. For everyone but the Caldicotts.

DELIA. Well, they have that barn of a house and the skittle alley and everything.

BRIGHT. Two fifty said.

BONWIT. Shout for anything you want.

HUGHSIE. All right.

(JENKINS comes in from the bar with IRENE's and LESTER's drinks. MARY-LOU sinks down on to the sofa next to IRENE.
HUGHSIE goes over and greets LUELLA and DWIGHT who return his greeting amiably but abstractedly.
DELIA helps herself to a cigarette from a box on a side-table.)

DELIA. *(While she lights her cigarette.)* Where's Louise?

LESTER. She'll be down in a minute. Mary-Lou — what are you drinking?

MARY-LOU. A dry martini — very dry indeed — Jenkins knows, don't you, Jenkins?

JENKINS. Yes, madam.

LESTER. Hughsie? Delia?
HUGHSIE. 'Old fashioned.'
DELIA. The same as Mary-Lou — dry martini — very dry.
JENKINS. Yes, madam.

(JENKINS leaves.)

DELIA. I don't hear any sounds of roaring — where's the new lion?

LESTER. He's not the roaring type —

HUGHSIE. I wonder if he plays squash.

LESTER. He doesn't *look* as if he did.

HUGHSIE. I've dated up the Schaefers' court for five thirty — want to play, Dwight?

DWIGHT. *(Looking up briefly from the backgammon table.)* Okay.

IRENE. Don't worry about me — I can always get Jenkins to read aloud to me. Nothing classic, you understand — just something light and soothing.

LESTER. How about *Life* magazine.

LUELLA. Too literary.

IRENE. You keep your mind on your dice, darling.

BRIGHT. *(Triumphantly.)* Four thousand five hundred.

BONWIT. God damn it!

(The conversation now becomes general.

LUELLA and DWIGHT have a slight argument about their backgammon.

BONWIT and BRIGHT EYES add up their scores.

MARY-LOU exchanges gossip with IRENE. LESTER, DELIA and HUGHSIE are discussing whether or not to go over to the Schaefers' for cocktails before dinner.

None of this dialogue is distinguishable because everyone is talking at once, the noise however is considerable.

At this moment, EVAN appears from the hall and stands for an instant transfixed with horror.
LESTER sees him and, with a scream, runs to him.)

LESTER. Evan! — My God, at last! I thought you were drowned!

(Everybody stops talking and looks up.)

BRIGHT. *(Still concentrating on the game.)* Fifteen hundred and two fifty to say.

LESTER. *(Taking EVAN's arm.)* I must introduce you to everybody. We'd better begin right here and work round the whole God-damned circle. *(Raises his voice.)* Listen, everyone — this is Evan Lorrimer — one of the greatest living English novelists, who shall be nameless — he's my friend and I'm crazy about him — *(To EVAN.)* — Aren't I, honey?

EVAN. *(Striving gallantly to overcome acute embarrassment.)* I really don't know.

LESTER. *(Leading him to the HUGHES HITCHCOCKS.)* This is Mr And Mrs Hughes Hitchcock — they live in a cosy little marble palazzo a couple of miles away. And their children! You've never seen such divine children! — I don't think they've ever seen them either.

DELIA. *(Smiling.)* Welcome to Long Island — you must come over and see us.

HUGHSIE. *(Shaking hands.)* Glad to see you over here.

LESTER. This is Bright Eyes Murphy gambling her poor broken life away. Bright Eyes — Mr Evan Lorrimer.

BRIGHT. *(Looking up with a smile.)* Hallo there — forgive me for not getting up but we're in the middle of a fight to the death.

BONWIT. *(Also looking up.)* Hallo, fellar — got everything you want?

EVAN. Yes, thank you.

BONWIT. Good for you — *(To BRIGHT.)* Four thousand five hundred.

BRIGHT. *(With vehemence.)* Rat! — I knew you'd get it.

LESTER. *(Dragging EVAN over to the backgammon table.)* This is Luella Rosen and Dwight Macadoo. Evan Lorrimer.

DWIGHT. *(Getting up.)* Hallo — how do you do.

EVAN. Please don't get up.

(DWIGHT sits down again.)

LUELLA. I'm crazy about your books, Mr Lorrimer — it's wonderful to have you over here.

EVAN. How kind of you — thank you very much.

DWIGHT. *(Politely.)* Do you play this game?

LUELLA. *(Rattling her dice.)* Come on, dice.

EVAN. Yes — when I was a little boy I used to play it with my grandmother.

DWIGHT. I expect the game's changed a bit since then.

LUELLA. Christ — double fives again.

EVAN. Yes — I think it has.

LESTER. This is Sergei Karinyenko. He's Russian — in a nice way.

SUKI. *(Rising and bowing politely.)* This is a great honour.

EVAN. Thanks — thanks very much.

LESTER. Mary-Lou — this is Mr Evan Lorrimer — the Countess Brancati. Her husband does the most sinister things in Italian diplomacy.

MARY-LOU. *(Shaking hands.)* We've all heard so much about you — it's lovely to meet you.

(The HUGHES HITCHCOCKS and SUKI drift into the bar.)

EVAN. You're very kind.

LESTER. And last — but by no means least — Irene Marlow —

Mr Evan Lorrimer. She's violently anti-British at the moment and in a hideous rage but it will all evaporate in a minute like clouds before the sun.

IRENE. Be quiet, Lester. Please don't pay any attention to him, Mr Lorrimer. I'm neither of those things.

EVAN. I'm so glad.

IRENE. *(Motioning him on to the sofa.)* Sit here — you must be exhausted having to meet so many strangers.

LESTER. I'll get you a drink and then I really must go and dress. Did you run a tub for me, dear?

EVAN. Yes — honey.

LESTER. *(Going into gales of laughter.)* There you are, you see! What did I tell you? He slays me.

(LESTER bounds off to the bar.)

IRENE. Lester's been telling us all about you and you've no idea how thrilled we are to meet you. I haven't read your book yet but I've got it.

LUELLA. *(Looking up from her game.)* Mr Lorrimer has written dozens of books, dear.

IRENE. Isn't Luella horrible? I'm never allowed to get away with a thing. Anyway, I meant your last one and I know it couldn't possibly matter to you whether I've read it or not but I really am longing to — particularly now that I've met you.

LUELLA. Irene's our pet moron — she's never read a book in her life except *The Thin Man* and *Stories of the Opera*. She's just an Iowa girl who's made good — aren't you darling?

IRENE. Listen, lamb pie — you leave Iowa out of this. What's the matter with Iowa, anyway?

LUELLA. You've been proving it to us for years.

(LESTER comes flying back from the bar with an 'old fashioned' which he hands to EVAN.)

LESTER. I've ordered more all round — they're on the way. I must fly — I won't be two minutes — thank God I've shaved — it used not to be necessary but I'm getting a big boy now. Don't anybody say anything important until I get back.

(LESTER runs out of the room and disappears in the direction of the stairs.)

MARY-LOU. He's sweet, Lester, isn't he? Everybody adores him.

EVAN. I'm sure they do.

IRENE. The vitality — it's fantastic! Did you see him in his show?

EVAN. Yes — Louise took me last night.

IRENE. It stinks, doesn't it?

EVAN. *(Startled.)* Well — I enjoyed it very much — it's the first American musical comedy I've seen.

IRENE. Well, don't let that put you off — we can do better than that. Didn't you think Lester was wonderful?

EVAN. Frightfully good.

IRENE. He shouldn't try to do that dance in the second act, though.

EVAN. Why not?

IRENE. He's past it. You can see he is. On the opening night it was sheer agony — I had to close my eyes and dig my nails into the palms of my hands.

EVAN. I thought he did it very well.

IRENE. He's been going a long time now, you know — I can remember him way back — when I was a little girl.

LUELLA. *(Over the back of the sofa.)* How little?

IRENE. About five foot seven. He was in *Johnny Head in Air*.

MARY-LOU. That was Fred Astaire.

IRENE. Not in Des Moines it wasn't. His voice isn't what it used to be either.

EVAN. *(Slightly irritated.)* I thought he sang very appealingly.

IRENE. That's all fake. There's no volume left — he has to force all the time. Too much gin.

(JENKINS appears with a tray of glasses.
IRENE and MARY-LOU put their empty glasses down and take fresh ones.)

JENKINS. Mr Lorrimer?

EVAN. No — thanks very much — I haven't finished this one yet.

IRENE. Better knock it back — you'll need it before the day's out.

EVAN. Really, I don't think —
IRENE. *(Firmly.)* Go on.
EVAN. *(Resigned.)* All right.

(He swallows his drink and takes another.).

IRENE. The same again, Jenkins.

EVAN. They're awfully strong.

MARY-LOU. I suppose England was terrible when you left, wasn't it? It usually is.

EVAN. *(Defensively.)* In what way?

MARY-LOU. We read such dreadful things here in the papers.

EVAN. Surely not only about England?

MARY-LOU. But you know what I mean, don't you? All the food rationing and the fuel situation and the Labour government? It *must* be depressing for you all. It couldn't possibly be anything else.

EVAN. *(Dryly.)* We're endeavouring to rise above it.

MARY-LOU. *(Enthusiastically.)* I think you're wonderful — the most wonderful people in the world. I always have thought so — haven't I, Irene?

IRENE. I don't know dear — I've only known you since 1944.

(HUGHSIE and DELIA come out of the bar and come over to the fireplace. DELIA sits in an armchair. HUGHSIE stands.)

HUGHSIE. How are you liking America, Mr Lorrimer?

EVAN. *(Relieved to be on safe ground again.)* Immensely. Of course I haven't seen much of it yet.

DELIA. You really must come and visit us — we're only two miles away from here.

EVAN. I should love to.

HUGHSIE. Make Louise bring you over.

DELIA. Or better still, why not come next weekend? There won't be anybody there but us. You can have your own sun-porch and work or rest or do anything you want to.

EVAN. It's most awfully kind of you but I'm afraid I can't. I leave for Boston on Wednesday to start my lecture tour.

DELIA. Isn't that extraordinary? All my family come from Boston.

EVAN. Really?

HUGHSIE. Delia was a Birdsall — before she married me.

EVAN. Oh yes, of course — I think Lester said something about it.

DELIA. You must meet my mother — she's a disaster.

HUGHSIE. We'll call her up tomorrow and tell her you're coming.

EVAN. Thank you very much.

DELIA. Do you think he'd like to stay with Aunt Evie? She'd adore it, of course.

HUGHSIE. I don't know whether he'd exactly *like* it, but it would certainly be an experience.

DELIA. She was one of the famous Cragley girls, you know. There were four of them and they all went mad except Aunt Evie.

HUGHSIE. And she's not far off it.

DELIA. But he ought to see it, oughn't he, Mary-Lou? I mean all that New England life — it's so apart from everything else. *(To EVAN.)* You've no idea what they're like — I mean you wouldn't believe it possible — that stiff-backed older generation, you know — for you as a writer it would be fascinating — they're all such formidable old characters.

IRENE. There's nothing gayer than a large group of formidable old characters.

DELIA. Now don't try to put him off, Irene. I'll call up Aunt Evie the moment I get back to the house.

HUGHSIE. Do you think he'd like the Van Leydens?

DELIA. Now, why didn't we think of that before?

IRENE. You're not properly warmed up yet — give yourselves time.

(JENKINS appears with another tray of drinks. Everyone has finished theirs but EVAN. They all put their empty glasses on the tray and take full ones. JENKINS looks at EVAN enquiringly, but with understanding.)

EVAN. No more for me, thank you.

MARY-LOU. But you *must* — mustn't he, Irene?

IRENE. Of *course* he must.

EVAN. I'm really not used to drinking in the middle of the day.

HUGHSIE. But this is *Sunday* — you must drink on Sunday. There's nothing else to do.

IRENE. That's nothing but ice water anyway.

(She firmly takes EVAN's glass from his hand, puts it on the tray and gives him a fresh one.)

EVAN. No, really —

(JENKINS exits.)

HUGHSIE. Come on — be a sport.

EVAN. It's going to my head already.

IRENE. Let it, dear — you're here to rest and relax.

EVAN. What time is lunch?

IRENE. I don't know — what time do they usually lunch? Dwight?

DWIGHT. *(Throwing the dice.)* I don't know — any old time.

EVAN. They?

MARY-LOU. The Darrells. We're all lunching with them — they're at Oyster Bay.

EVAN. Where's that?

IRENE. *(Soothingly.)* Quite near.

HUGHSIE. It's just the other side of Manhasset.

EVAN. Oh, I see.

MARY-LOU. Do you mean to say you've never met Fabia Darrell?

EVAN. I don't think so.

MARY-LOU. She was at our embassy in London before the war.

HUGHSIE. Before that she was in Shanghai.

IRENE. She's a darling — but terribly energetic.

MARY-LOU. He's extraordinary, too — you'll be fascinated.

EVAN. *(Lifting his glass. Loudly.)* The Darrells! *(He drains it.)*

(At this moment a diversion is caused by the arrival of LEONIE CRANE and SHIRLEY BENEDICT. They are both attractive with rather close cut hair. They are both wearing skiing clothes and small pearl button earrings.)

LEONIE. *(Gaily.)* Hallo everybody! Are we late? I though we'd never get here.

SHIRLEY. *(As they advance into the room.)* We had a flat tyre and had to get a man from the Lawford's garage.

LEONIE. We've been practising skiing out beyond Isabel's — I'm exhausted.

SHIRLEY. *(On the steps of the bar.)* Two short sharp martinis, Jenkins — we're in dire distress.

JENKINS. *(Off.)* Yes, Miss Benedict.

SHIRLEY. I suppose it would cause talk if I married Jenkins.

LEONIE. I suspect Jenkins might have something to say about it. So might I, come to that!

(LESTER comes flying in dressed like an advertisement for country clothes in Esquire. *He embraces LEONIE and SHIRLEY enthusiastically.)*

LESTER. It can't be true, that's all — it just can't possibly be true – I heard your voices in the hall and I couldn't believe my ears. Why aren't you in Arizona?

LEONIE. We got sick of it.

LESTER. How was Martha?

SHIRLEY. Quite awful and drinking too much.

LEONIE. *(Sharply.)* Shirley!

SHIRLEY. It's true and you know it.

LESTER. My dears, we must steal away into some little rose-covered pergola and you must tell me all — I can't wait.

LEONIE. There's nothing to tell.

LESTER. Anyway, what are you both doing dressed as Gregory Peck?

SHIRLEY. We've been skiing.

LESTER. Evan, quickly — come here but at once! *(EVAN rises from the sofa and comes across the room.)* This is Leonie Crane and this is Shirley Benedict — Evan Lorrimer. I'm here to tell you that when you've known these two belles for two minutes you'll never leave them again until the grave closes over you.

SHIRLEY. How are you, Mr Lorrimer?

(SHIRLEY wrings his hand manfully.)

LESTER. Leonie's written three plays herself. And she adores everything you've ever done.

LEONIE. *(Also wringing his hand.)* Lester exaggerates so — but I did think *A Lady of London* was swell. Shirley and I read it in Capri in the summer.

EVAN. *(Correcting her.) A London Lady.*

LEONIE. *(Laughing with embarrassment.)* That's typical of me — I've never got a name right in my life.

LESTER. *(To EVAN.)* Having a good time, honey?

EVAN. *(With rather an amateur wave of the hand.)* Out of this world!

(EVAN giggles.)

LESTER. *(Laughing happily.)* Isn't he to die for?

(JENKINS appears with a tray loaded with drinks.
LEONIE and SHIRLEY take theirs.
LESTER takes two 'old fashioneds' — one for himself and one for EVAN, who accepts it without protest.
At this moment LOUISE appears with a great cry.)

LOUISE. Darlings! Can you ever forgive me — I'm so ashamed I could kill myself — I've had poor Nancy on the telephone wailing at me for hours — she's in absolute despair — Babe's gone flying off to Nassau with that scheming little Pop Hardacre and Nancy's suicidal — but seriously — I hadn't the heart to cut her off — on she went sobbing and moaning — Why do people always have to come to me with all their confidences — it makes me so *late* for everything. *(SUKI enters out of the bar. LOUISE goes up to EVAN and takes both his hands in hers.)* You'll never forgive me — I feel terribly, terribly guilty. Did you sleep well? Has Lester been looking after you all right? Have you met everybody?

LESTER. Don't fuss, darling — everything's under control.

LOUISE. But we must leave at once — everybody. *(She raises her voice.)* We *must* leave this instant — Fabia will never forgive me — Evan — you come with me — Leonie — Shirley — how lovely to see you — you take Suki with you. Irene will you and Dwight take the people you came with? Hughsie and Delia, be angelic and take any left-overs you see loitering about — Come along, Bonny — Bright Eyes — I didn't know you were here!

BONWIT. We'll come later, dear. We have to finish this game.

BRIGHT. Fabia doesn't expect me, anyway.

BONWIT. We'll stay here then — Jenkins can make us a sandwich.

BRIGHT. That's okay with me.

LOUISE. You really are too tiresome, both of you.

LESTER. *(To EVAN.)* Cheer up, sweetie pie — you're going to the most fabulous house on Long Island. It's the biggest thing since *Ben Hur*.

LOUISE. It's unbelievable what they've done to that house — really unbelievable.

EVAN. I think — if you don't mind very much — I won't come.

LOUISE. *(Shocked.)* But, my dear, you *must*.

EVAN. I'd really rather not — I want to make a few notes for my first lecture and —

LOUISE. *(Pleading.)* Please — *please* come. The Darrells will be so bitterly disappointed, they're pining to meet you and they're such darlings.

EVAN. *(Firmly.)* I really would prefer to stay here.

LESTER. Then I won't go either.

LOUISE. Neither will I — we'll none of us go — I'll telephone them right away.

LESTER. They're awfully sweet people — they really are —

she's from the Deep South — You really ought to meet *someone* from the Deep South while you're here.

LOUISE. Don't worry him, Lester, if he'd rather not. We'll have a picnic lunch here — I'll tell Jenkins.

EVAN. Why can't you all go without me?

LOUISE. My dear, I wouldn't dream of it — besides, they'd never speak to me again. Fabia's been on the telephone ever since she heard that you were coming —

LESTER. You'll worship her — you really will.

EVAN. *(Giving in.)* Very well — we can come back directly after lunch, can't we?

LOUISE. You're an angel! Of course we can — we won't even wait for coffee. *(To LESTER.)* We'd better go by the state highway and turn left by the bridge on account of the snow.

LESTER. If we do we shall arrive at the Witherspoons — and God forbid we should do that.

LOUISE. Nonsense — the Witherspoons are right over on the other side near the Caldicotts.

LESTER. It would be much better to go up that turning just past the Obermeyer's gate, then on over the hill and turn right at the cross-roads.

LOUISE. *Left* at the cross-roads — if you turn right at the cross-roads you come straight to the golf course and that's miles away — just next to the Schaeffers —

LESTER. You're out of your mind, darling — the Schaeffers are in the opposite direction entirely!

LUELLA. Is it true that Minnie Schaeffer is going to have another baby?

LESTER. She *can't* be!

IRENE. Judging by the look of it she didn't *quite* have the last one.

LESTER. *(To LOUISE.)* Haven't you got a map?

LOUISE. I don't need a map — I know the way blindfolded.

LESTER. Once we get off the State Highway we're in trouble — I warn you — look what happened last time.

LOUISE. That was only because you insisted on taking that short cut by the Hubermans.

LESTER. I did not.

LOUISE. Don't be so stubborn, Lester. You know you have no bump of locality.

IRENE. One step out of Forty-Second Street and the robins cover him with leaves.

LUELLA. Dwight knows the way anyhow — you can follow us.

IRENE. That'll be dicing with death.

LOUISE. *(Squeezing EVAN's arm affectionately.)* You're a darling to say you'll come — I really do appreciate it.

LESTER. I swear you won't regret it — particularly if old Sophie Darrell's there – she's sensational – stone deaf and looks like a bull-moose!

EVAN. How nice.

DWIGHT. I'll go and start the car. *(To IRENE.)* Are you ready?

IRENE. Just mulling over my last words.

LOUISE. Come along — come along, everybody — we must fly like the wind!

(LOUISE and LESTER drag EVAN out into the hall. They are followed by everybody, chattering and laughing.

The noise continues in the hall for a little and dies away with the noise of cars starting in the drive.)

BONWIT. Saying two-fifty

CURTAIN

ACT II

Scene 1

(The guest-room. About four-thirty in the afternoon.

When the curtain rises, the room is empty. After a moment or two
 EVAN comes in. He is wearing a large overcoat and muffler and
 a hat, and he looks and walks, a trifle unsteadily, over to the
 fireplace and looks anxiously in the mirror over the mantelpiece.
 He takes off his hat and throws it on the bed He scrutinises his
 face, pulls down one of his eyes and shudders, then shakes his
 head violently two or three times. This obviously makes him feel
 giddy so he sits down on the bed. He sits there unhappily for a
 moment and then, with a great effort, gets up and takes off his
 overcoat and muffler. These he flings on to the chaise-longue.
 They miss the chaise-longue and fall down behind it, but he is
 past caring.

Suddenly a thought strikes him. He opens the door cautiously and
 listens, then tiptoes into the bathroom, returning in a moment
 with a bottle of aspirin. He pours out some water from the carafe
 by his bed, shakes three aspirin into the palm of his hand and
 swallows them. He then wearily undoes his shoes and takes them
 off and lies on his bed.

There is a sharp knock on the door. He jumps and gives a slight groan.)

EVAN. *(Huskily.)* Come in.

(LESTER comes in, and, seeing him stretched out on the bed, gives a little cry of commiseration.)

LESTER. I came to see if you were all right.

EVAN. Thanks very much.

LESTER. Are you?

EVAN. Am I what?

LESTER. All right?

EVAN. No.

LESTER. *(Sympathetically. Sitting on EVAN's bed.)* What's the matter, dear?

EVAN. *(Testily.)* Nothing's the matter. I just don't feel very well.

LESTER. Do you think it was those clams at lunch?

EVAN. No, I don't.

LESTER. *(Resting his hand on EVAN's forehead.)* You haven't got a fever.

EVAN. I know I haven't got a fever.

LESTER. Does your head ache?

EVAN. Yes, it does.

LESTER. Why not take some aspirin?

EVAN. I have.

LESTER. I think I will, too.

EVAN. Do, by all means.

LESTER. Where are they?

EVAN. *(Indicating them.)* Here, on the table.

LESTER. *(Pouring himself out some water.)* I've got a headache too.

EVAN. *(With an edge in his voice.)* I'm so sorry.

LESTER. *(Swallowing two aspirin.)* What we both need is forty winks.

EVAN. I quite agree.

LESTER. I've always thought Fabia Darrell was a tiresome bitch and I still think so — don't you?

EVAN. I don't know which she was.

LESTER. Your hostess, dear. You sat on her right at lunch.

EVAN. Oh — that one!

LESTER. The one on your other side was Sue Pendelton.

EVAN. Was it, indeed?

LESTER. Didn't you think she was heaven?

EVAN. I don't remember.

LESTER. She was married to Bugsie Halliwell at first, then he lost everything in the 1929 crash and flung himself off the Fifty-ninth Street bridge.

EVAN. *(Grimly.)* How wise.

LESTER. Then she married Doc Pendelton who's worth millions but they fought like steers and she cracked him over the head with a bottle one night at the El Morocco and so he divorced her and now she's at a loose end.

EVAN. I'm not surprised.

LESTER. She's perfectly all right as long as she sticks to light wines and beer. It's hard liquor that fixes her. You'd never believe it — she becomes a different woman under your very eyes — split personality, you know —

EVAN. *(Crossly.)* No, I don't know.

LESTER. Am I boring you?

EVAN. Yes.

LESTER. *(Contrite.)* Honey, why didn't you *say*? — I'll go away and leave you alone this very minute — I'm an inconsiderate son-of-a-bitch.

EVAN. *(A little ashamed.)* It's only that I've got a headache and want to go to sleep.

LESTER. I could kick myself — really I could.

EVAN. There's no necessity for that.

LESTER. How long do you want to sleep?

EVAN. For ever.

LESTER. You really are wonderful! You never lose your sense

of humour, do you?

EVAN. There are moments when it becomes rather submerged. This is one of them.

LESTER. Everybody's crazy about you. You know that, don't you?

EVAN. No.

LESTER. You should have heard the way they were all carrying on after lunch when you'd gone to the Lulu. My dear, you're the biggest hit since *Oklahoma*.

EVAN. Good.

LESTER. You've got Irene positively writhing at your feet! That's no mean achievement, I can tell you.

EVAN. Do go away now, Lester — please.

LESTER. I'm on my way. *(Pats EVAN's hand.)* Why don't you take your coat and trousers off?

EVAN. I don't want to.

LESTER. I always believe in slipping right *in* to bed.

EVAN. I'd rather stay as I am, if you don't mind.

LESTER. They'll get all mussed up.

EVAN. What will?

LESTER. Your trousers.

EVAN. I don't care if they do.

LESTER. *(Worried.)* You ought to have something over you — here — I'll whisk the coverlet off the other bed.

(LESTER takes the coverlet off the other bed and spreads it over EVAN.)

EVAN. Thanks.
LESTER. Comfy?
EVAN. Yes.
LESTER. I'll draw the curtains.
EVAN. Thanks.

LESTER. *(Drawing the curtains.)* You know there's trouble brewing, don't you?

EVAN. No.

LESTER. Hughsie and Louise were having a heart-to-heart in the ping-pong room before lunch and Delia found them. Didn't you notice her face afterwards — it was like thunder? I tried to catch your eye. They'll be a bust-up soon or my name's not Emily Post. *(EVAN doesn't answer. LESTER tiptoes to the door.)* Sleep well, honey — I'll call you if anything happens.

(LESTER goes out and closes the door quietly behind him.

EVAN waits for a moment and then flings off the coverlet and goes over to the door and locks it. He gets back on to the bed again and draws the coverlet over him, heaves a deep sigh and buries his head in the pillow.

After a slight pause there is a gentle tap at the door.

EVAN starts up and listens. He waits, then it comes again, more insistently. With a muttered curse he gets up and opens the door. LOUISE comes in.)

LOUISE. *(Speaking softly.)* I just came to see if you were all right.

EVAN. Perfectly all right, thanks — I was just having a little rest.

LOUISE. *(With her fingers to her lips.)* Shhh! Don't speak loudly, Lester's asleep and we mustn't wake him. *(She closes the door gently and switches on the lights.)* Are you quite sure you've got everything you want?

EVAN. Quite sure, thanks.

LOUISE. *(Sinking on to the chaise-longue.)* I'm absolutely exhausted.

EVAN. So am I.

LOUISE. Aren't people extraordinary? I mean, the way they have no idea of doing things properly — that lunch party, for instance —

Fabia must be raving and — it couldn't have been more boring and the food was uneatable. I do apologise — I had no idea it was going to be so deadly.

EVAN. It certainly was rather crowded.

LOUISE. She swore to me on her solemn oath that it was just going to be ourselves. When we arrived and I saw all those hordes of people, I was mortified — I really was — and why in the world do you suppose did she have to invite those awful Leatherwicks.

EVAN. I don't know which they were.

LOUISE. Cora Leatherwick was the one with the tortured mauve hair and the rasping voice. The daughter was sitting opposite to you at lunch — a vast, freckled girl with glasses who never stops talking for a moment. The hairy young man next to her with the big Adam's apple is her fiancé. He never utters.

EVAN. They ought to be happy.

LOUISE. Well, they'll be very rich at any rate. He's one of the Crombies, you know — worth millions — Crombie Cow Cakes.

EVAN. No — I didn't know.

LOUISE. Do you mind if I have just one cigarette and then I'll leave you in peace — I really am quite shattered?

EVAN. *(Miserably.)* Of course.

(He hands her a cigarette box and she takes one.)

LOUISE. This *is* a lovely quiet room, isn't it?
EVAN. *(Lighting her cigarette for her.)* Lovely.
LOUISE. *(Leaning back and inhaling luxuriously.)* That's better.
EVAN. *(Resigned.)* I might as well have one too.

(He helps himself to a cigarette.).

LOUISE. I don't smoke much as a general rule — just every now and then when I feel jittery — it's wonderfully soothing.

EVAN. I hope you're right.

(He lights his cigarette and sits mournfully on the bed.)

LOUISE. *(Pensively.)* You are an extraordinary person, you know — but then I always knew you would be.

EVAN. In what way — extraordinary?

LOUISE. Well, you're utterly human to begin with. And you have such a wealth of understanding — one feels it when one is talking to you — you give people a sense of security.

EVAN. I'm sure it's very sweet of you to say so.

LOUISE. Oh, I'm not being sweet, I assure you. When you get to know me a little better you'll realise that I *never* flatter people — on the contrary, I'm often accused of being just the other way. Withdrawn and remote and over-fastidious.

EVAN. I haven't found you in the least withdrawn.

LOUISE. Ah, that's because I like you. I felt the first moment that I talked to you that we were old friends. *(She sighs.)* I have very few friends — thousands of acquaintances, of course, but friends — that's a different matter, isn't it?

EVAN. Yes.

LOUSE. I find that people give awfully little, don't you?

EVAN. I prefer it to them giving too much.

LOUISE. That was cynical. Would you describe yourself as a cynic?

EVAN. I very seldom describe myself at all.

LOUISE. I don't think you're a cynic. You may use cynicism as a mask occasionally, but underneath you have a tremendously kind heart. I'm sure of it.

EVAN. *(Forcing a grateful smile.)* Thank you.

LOUISE. It must be frightening sometimes — knowing people inside out — watching all their little faults and failings.

EVAN. I don't think I do.

LOUISE. *(Firmly.)* You must. Otherwise you couldn't possibly write the things you write or be the person you rare. Incidentally, you look perfectly wretched sitting on the edge of the bed like that — why don't you put your feet up and relax?

EVAN. Thanks — I will.

(He moves over and climbs on to his own bed and props the pillow behind his head.)

LOUISE. That's better, isn't it? There should be an ash-tray just by you.

EVAN. There is.

LOUISE. *(After a slight pause.)* Would you say — offhand — that I was a happy woman?

EVAN. *(Startled.)* It's difficult to decide on those sort of things — offhand.

LOUISE. It's not difficult for anyone with a mind like yours, so it's no use pretending it is.

EVAN. What do you want me to say?

LOUISE. What you think. What you truly and honestly think.

EVAN. *(Tactfully.)* I think that if you're not happy, you certainly put up a magnificent façade.

LOUISE. *(Wistfully.)* That's very dear of you — and very kind.

EVAN. I would be wary of jumping to conclusions on such a short acquaintance.

LOUISE. *(With simple directness.)* What would you do if you were married to Bonwit?

EVAN. I don't know. Such a contingency hadn't occurred to me.

LOUISE. I'm devoted to Bonwit — there isn't a thing in the world I wouldn't do for him.

EVAN. I'm sure there isn't.

LOUISE. But we happen to inhabit different planets. We're utterly apart from each other, in every way.

EVAN. I see.

LOUISE. Oh, I wonder if you do, really.

EVAN. Why are you telling me all this?

LOUISE. *(With a break in her voice.)* Because I need help — I'm in desperate trouble.

EVAN. *(Panic-stricken.)* I'm most awfully sorry.

LOUISE. *(Rising and going over to the window and drawing back the curtain.)* Last night when you were standing here looking at the moon shining down on to the sea and you were quoting Shelley so beautifully.

EVAN. Matthew Arnold.

LOUISE. I suddenly had an impulse to tear open the window and throw myself out, down and away.

EVAN. I'm very glad you didn't obey it.

LOUISE. *(With a little laugh.)* My sense of humour saved me. I suddenly realised that I should merely fall on to the sun porch.

EVAN. I must say you gave me no indication that you were in such distress.

LOUISE. I know you think I'm a fool and that I'm exaggerating everything, but I really am dreadfully unhappy and I don't know what to do.

(She bursts into tears.)

EVAN. *(Jumping up.)* Louise — don't — please don't —

(He puts his arm round her shoulder.)

LOUISE. It's all right — I shall feel better in a minute.

EVAN. What can I do to help?

LOUISE. Nothing, really — I just felt that I had to confide in somebody — please forgive me and lie down again.

EVAN. But Louise —

LOUISE. Lie down again, please — I insist — I'll never forgive myself if you don't — you're here for a rest.

EVAN. Very well.

(He lies down on the bed again.)

LOUISE. *(Gently.)* Close your eyes — I don't want you to look at me while I say what I'm going to say —

EVAN. Don't you think you'd better wait a little — before you tell me anything you may regret?

LOUISE. I'd never regret telling you anything — I trust you absolutely.

EVAN. But Louise — really — you've had an exhausting lunch party and you're obviously nervy and over-strung. Don't you think you'd better go and lie down for a while and think everything over calmly?

LOUISE. *(In tears again.)* I can't think anymore — it's all too much for me — I can't think any more — please close your eyes.

EVAN. *(Wearily.)* Very well.

(He does so.
LOUISE takes another cigarette, lights it and begins to walk up and down the room.
EVAN opens his eyes and looks at her, shudders and closes them again.)

LOUISE. *(Quietly, in a sad, reminiscent voice.)* I was only a girl when I married my first husband — we lived — my parents and I — in the country, not far from Detroit — it was lovely in those days — that flat, limitless prairie land — it's all changed now, of course — but then everything changes, doesn't it?

(She pauses.)

EVAN. *(Opening his eyes.)* Yes.

(He closes his eyes again.)

LOUISE. Ed — that was his name, Ed Tinklor — Ed was a sweet boy when I first knew him — a typical clean-living young American full of ambition and ideas — I, of course, was absurdly young and didn't know anything about anything. We were very happy for years until he began to make money and we moved to Chicago and then to New York. After that everything went wrong. I was just as much to blame as he was really, I suppose — I see that now — but then I was young and self-willed and, I suppose, pretty ruthless — incidentally it was just about that time that I first met Lester. He was playing quite a small part in *Good Gracious* at the New Amsterdam.

EVAN. *(Opening his eyes.) Good Gracious*?

LOUISE. It was a lovely show — I remember it distinctly — He was quite a young boy then. *He's* changed too.

EVAN. Like the limitless prairie.

(He closes his eyes drowsily.).

LOUISE. Sometime after that I met Bonwit. I had divorced Ed and I was lonely and unsure. He, Bonwit, fell in love with me — he kept on begging and begging me to marry him and finally I did. We went to Europe for our honeymoon — it was the first time I'd ever been to Europe — I shall never forget it — We took a house in London for the season — dear old London — that's why I shall always love it whatever happens — because I was so happy there. We went to Paris too and Venice and Rome and all over everywhere. It didn't take me long to realise, of course, that although Bonwit was an angel and kindness itself and actually worshipped the ground I walked on, that really — deep down — we were poles apart. I don't blame him — I'd never blame Bonwit for anything. How was he to know that there was something secret in me — something so secret that I didn't even realise it myself — a sort of indefinable longing? *(She pauses and looks at EVAN. His eyes are closed.)* It wasn't until years and years and years later that suddenly — just on an ordinary day just like any other day — I realised the truth. I had never been in love at all. Never in my whole life. I had been fond of Ed, in an unthinking, immature way. I was fond of Bonwit, as I still am, but Love! I'd never even remotely experienced it, never even touched the hem of its garment. Then of course, Fate intervened — as it always does – and I met Hughsie. That did it. The spark was struck once and for all and there was no going back. I shall never love anyone else in my life but him as long as I live. I knew that in the beginning. In spite of everything and because of everything Hughsie is to me and always will be, the most attractive man I've ever known. And now — when it's too late and he's married to Delia, who won't let him out of her sight for an instant — Now — at long at last — he realises his mistake — *(She starts to weep again.)* — Don't you see, Evan — dear, kind, understanding man that you are — don't you see why I'm in such despair — such utter, utter despair? *(She pauses and looks at EVAN again. She raises her voice a little.)* Evan! — *(Then, a trifle more sharply.)* Evan !! *(She proceeds to shake him by the shoulder. He grunts a little and his head falls back. She stands looking down at him twisting her handkerchief in rage and frustration.)* Damned drunken idiot!

(She stamps out of the room slamming the door violently behind her. EVAN wakes up with a start.)

EVAN. Good gracious!

(He looks sleepily round the room — sees that it is empty — heaves a sigh of relief and goes to sleep again.
The lights fade.)

Scene 2

(The lights fade in.

EVAN is sound asleep. The door opens quietly and LESTER comes in. He is followed by DON LUCAS, a tall, excessively handsome young man with the mark of Hollywood indelibly branded upon him. He carries a Scotch highball. LESTER carries two.)

LESTER. Switch on the light — my hands are full.

DON. *(Doing so.)* Okay.

LESTER. *(Putting the drinks carefully on the bedside table.)* There.

DON. Has he passed out or is he just asleep?

LESTER. *Ca c'est un moot point* — as the French laughingly say.

DON. It seems a shame to wake the poor guy.

LESTER. *(Meditatively.)* I always think people look defenceless when they're asleep, don't you? — It's the great pulsating mother's heart in me.

DON. He's certainly 'out' in a big way.

LESTER. I wonder if he's dreaming. It's fascinating to imagine what goes on in a creative mind like that when it's asleep.

DON. Sex, I expect. That's what Frood says.

LESTER. Not Frood, dear — Freud.

DON. Have it your on way.

LESTER. *(Looking at EVAN affectionately.)* I'll bet his subconscious is sensational!

DON. He's drooling a bit, isn't he?

LESTER. People always drool when they sleep in the daytime. It's on account of their salivary glands — which shall be nameless.

DON. *(Interested.)* No fooling?

LESTER. Wait till he sees you — Don Lucas himself — in the

flesh! He'll have a fit.

DON. *(Complacently, giving a quick glance in the mirror.)* Could be.

LESTER. *(Shaking EVAN's shoulder gently.)* Evan — *(EVAN grunts.)* Evan — wake up, honey.

DON. I always lash out when anybody does that to me.

LESTER. But you're the primitive type, dear — in practically every way.

DON. *(Amiably.)* Nuts!

LESTER. *(Shaking EVAN harder.)* Evan — wake up.

EVAN. *(Opening his eyes.)* What is it?

LESTER. You've been asleep for hours.

EVAN. *(Foggily.)* What's the time?

LESTER. It's after six.

EVAN. *(With great effort.)* Please make my apologies to Mrs Steinhauser and say that I feel far from well and would like to rest a little — *(He suddenly remembers.)* Good God!

LESTER. What's the matter?

EVAN. Louise! Where is she?

LESTER. Playing ping-pong.

EVAN. She was here a minute ago.

LESTER. Oh no, she wasn't. That's your treacherous subconscious playing you up.

EVAN. *(Suddenly seeing DON for the first time.)* Oh!

LESTER. Do you realise who this is?

EVAN. No — I'm afraid I don't.

LESTER. Don Lucas.

EVAN. How do you do?

DON. Glad to know you, sir.

LESTER. *The* Don Lucas.

EVAN. Are there many?

LESTER. *(Laughing.)* There you are, you see? What did I tell you? Isn't he wonderful?

DON. You'll have to forgive me — busting into your room like this — Lester made me.

EVAN. *(Dimly.)* Not at all — I'm delighted — make yourself at home.

LESTER. Don's on a three weeks vacation from Hollywood. He's just finished making *The Loves of Cardinal Richelieu* for Paramount and he's going back on Thursday to start work on *Samovar* for MGM.

EVAN. I see.

DON. It's based on *War and Peace* by Gorky.

LESTER. Dostoevsky, dear.

EVAN. *(Wearily.)* Balzac!

DON. It's going to be a swell picture anyway. They're trying to get Opal Dawn.

LESTER. My God!

DON. It will be her first non-singing picture.

LESTER. Oh no, it won't!

DON. You've always been bitchy about Opal — I think she's terrific.

LESTER. All right, sweetheart. I'll take the high road and you take the low road.

DON. How d'you mean?

LESTER. Skip it.

DON. She's better than Jean Hazel anyway.

LESTER. So's Prussic acid. *(To EVAN.)* We've brought you a drink.

EVAN. *(Groaning.)* Oh, no!

LESTER. *(handing him a Scotch highball.)* Go on — it will do you good.

EVAN. I couldn't — I really couldn't.

DON. Come on — be a sport.

EVAN. *(Irritably.)* It's not a question of being a sport. I just don't want any more to drink.

LESTER. You'll feel like death the whole evening long if you don't.

EVAN. I shall feel like death anyhow.

LESTER. How's your headache?

EVAN. Very bad indeed.

LESTER. *(Persuasively.)* Take a sip of this — it'll make all the difference — I swear it will.

EVAN. No.

LESTER. Come on — there's a good boy.

EVAN. You're mad you know — all of you — stark staring *mad*.

LESTER. *(Admonishingly.)* Temper — temper!

EVAN. What on earth did you wake me up for — I think it was most inconsiderate.

LESTER. Irene's going to sing.

EVAN. What's that got to do with it?

LESTER. Everything. She's going to sing for *you*.

EVAN. I'm sure it's very kind of her but —

LESTER. She's taken a mad shine to you and says she won't open her trap unless you come and sit right by the piano. You'll ruin the whole thing if you don't come — Louise will be dreadfully upset.

EVAN. Louise seems to have a very volatile temperament.

LESTER. Irene's really sensational when she sings. I swear I wouldn't try to persuade you unless I knew that you'd adore it.

EVAN. *(Hopelessly.) Right* by the piano?

LESTER. Yes.

EVAN. Give me that drink.

(He grabs the drink from LESTER's hand and drains half of it.).

LESTER. Atta baby!

EVAN. *(Choking slightly and staggering up from the bed.)* If you'll excuse me I think I should like to go to the bathroom for a minute.

LESTER. It's all yours, honey.
EVAN. *(Weakly.)* Thanks — thanks very much.

(He goes out of the room and into the bathroom. He slams the bathroom door.).

DON. He seems a nice guy.
LESTER. He's a bit under the weather now, poor sweet, but just you wait — he'll be a riot later on.
DON. Fancy anyone like that writing all those god-damned books! I can't understand it.
LESTER. Press on, dear boy — you can't expect too much at first.

(There is the sound of voices in the passage and LUELLA's voice calling.)

LUELLA. Lester — Lester — where the hell are you?
LESTER. Come right in, darling, everything's depressingly above board.

(LUELLA comes in.)

LUELLA. Surprise — surprise! Who do you think's here?

(She stands aside and CAROLA BINNEY comes in followed by BOB and GLORIA HOCKBRIDGE.
CAROLA radiates charm, personality and vitality. She is one of the most famous light comediennes in the American theatre.
BOB is a short, square man with glasses. He is one of the better known playwrights.
GLORIA, his wife, is decorative. She wears rather barbaric clothes and her blonde hair is worn like Joan of Arc. She is an

outstanding theatrical designer of costumes and décor.)

LESTER. *(With a scream.)* Carola! Of all people! It's not possible! It's just a great big wonderful dream! *(They fly into each other's arms.)* Bob! — Gloria! I haven't seen you since Mrs Lesley Carter swung around on that old bell!

CAROLA. Darling — you look fine! Hallo, Don – I heard you were in town. I've been rehearsing like crazy and I haven't been out anywhere.

(They kiss affectionately.)

LESTER. Gloria — Bob — you both know Don Lucas, don't you?
BOB. Yes — we've seen Grant's Tomb, too.
DON. Hallo there.
GLORIA. Your last picture was the best thing you ever did, Don — I was a sodden mass.
BOB. *(Bouncing on EVAN's bed.)* Well this feels like home — twin beds and the parlour full of Spaniards!
CAROLA. Where's the English writer?
LESTER. In the turlet.
BOB. I call that downright human and unaffected of him. He must have the Common Touch.
LESTER. He's divine — you'll worship him.
BOB. I worship all English writers on principle.
GLORIA. *(Looking round the room appraisingly.)* If I were Louise, I'd send those curtains right back where they came from.
LUELLA. Perhaps she doesn't know.
CAROLA. Who all's here, Lester? Luella caught us in the hall when we arrived and rushed us straight to find you.
LESTER. Practically everybody but Garbo and the Trumans.
BOB. Nice work.

CAROLA. *(Noticing EVAN's coat behind the chaise-lounge.)* What's this?

LESTER. Sweetie-pie's coat — he's very untidy — I really shall have to speak to him.

CAROLA. *(Picking it up and sniffing it.)* It's wonderful tweed — I'm queer for men's overcoats anyway. *(Puts it on.)* How do I look?

LESTER. Like Jackie Coogan in the dear old silent days. *(At this moment EVAN emerges from the bathroom. He looks slightly revived, but the top two buttons of his trousers are undone and he is carrying his coat. He stands transfixed with horror in the doorway. LESTER runs to him.)* Feeling better, dear?

EVAN. Yes, thank you.

LESTER. This is Carola Binney — even if you haven't heard of Abraham Lincoln, you must have heard of *her*!

EVAN. How do you do.

CAROLA. I'm thrilled to meet you, Mr Lorrimer. *(Stricken.)* Oh dear — this is your overcoat, isn't it?

EVAN. *(With a forced smile.)* Yes – as a matter of fact, it is.

CAROLA. I just saw it lying there and put it on.

EVAN. You look charming in it.

CAROLA. It's wonderful tweed — I adore tweeds.

EVAN. Yes — they are nice, aren't they?

CAROLA. I think I'd better let you have it back, hadn't I?

(She takes it off and puts it on the chaise-lounge.).

EVAN. I don't need it for a moment — it's quite warm in here.

CAROLA. A husband of mine used to have the most beautiful tweed sent to him from Dumfries.

EVAN. This conversation might lead almost anywhere, mightn't it?

LESTER. Oh Bob — this is Evan Lorrimer — Bob Hockbridge.

EVAN. Robert Hockbridge — the dramatist?

BOB. I'm your man.

LESTER. You must have seen his play in London — it was a smash hit — *Study of a Murderess* all about Charlotte Corday.

EVAN. *(Palpably embarrassed.)* Yes — yes, indeed I did.

BOB. I expect you thought I'd taken a few liberties with history?

EVAN. Well, I must say I never realised that she had killed so many other men besides Marat.

LESTER. This is Gloria Hockbridge. Don't be deceived by her mystic appearance. She's about as dreamy as a cash register.

EVAN. How do you do.

GLORIA. *(Shaking hands.)* Welcome to America. Lester's introductions are rather startling, aren't they?

EVAN. Yes — they certainly are.

LESTER. Far be it from me to discourage any spirit of breezy optimism but the top buttons of your pants are undone.

EVAN. *(Through clenched teeth.)* I know they are.

LESTER. Do them up at once, dear — mother's ashamed.

EVAN. Thank you — I will.

(EVAN throws his coat on the bed and does so.).

CAROLA, Is this your first time in the States, Mr Lorrimer?

EVAN. Yes — I arrived last Wednesday.

CAROLA. How are you enjoying it?

EVAN. *(Manfully.)* Immensely — of course, I haven't seen much as yet.

CAROLA. I always think the first view of New York from the sea is tremendously impressive — that skyline —

BOB. The champagne air has its points too.

CAROLA. Shut up, Bob.

LESTER. I'm going to rustle up some drinks — shan't be a minute — come on Don.

(LESTER and DON run out. EVAN looks after them hopelessly.)

CAROLA. You must think it awful of us to invade your bedroom like this, Mr Lorrimer?

EVAN. *(With a wan smile.)* Not at all — I'm delighted.

CAROLA. Do sit down, won't you? You look so uncomfortable.

EVAN. Thanks.

(He sits on the bed.)

LUELLA. How's the new play, Carola?

CAROLA. Ask Bob — he wrote it.

BOB. It's coming along fine — it will be better when Carola knows her lines.

CAROLA. *(Waiting.)* It's no use bullying me — you know I'm a slow study, I always have been. (To EVAN.) Ninety-three sides — imagine!

EVAN. *(Out of his depth.)* Imagine!

CAROLA. I'm on the stage from the whole time from the beginning of the first act until the end of the last — gobbling away like a turkey.

EVAN. *(Inadequately.)* It must be very tiring.

CAROLA. Tiring! I shall be flat on my back in the Doctor's Hospital if we run longer than three weeks. It's worse than *The Red Thrush Vanishes*.

EVAN. What was that?

CAROLA. A play I did two seasons ago for the Guild. It reeked of the soil — I had to play the whole second act perched up on a goddamned tractor with an idiot farmhand.

EVAN. Was it a success?

CAROLA. No. I don't know *what* it was quite – but it lacked something.

BOB. I know what it lacked all right — Rodgers, Hammerstein

and Agnes de Mille.
EVAN. Who are they?

(Everybody roars with laughter.)

CAROLA. *(Wiping her eyes.)* I can't bear it — I know I can't bear it —I'd much better die here and now and save everyone a great deal of trouble!

LUELLA. How are you getting along with Brod Lawton?

CAROLA. My dear, I'm crazy about him — he's a genius — the best director I ever had in my life. He acts every single scene out for me — it's fascinating — I sit there at the side of the stage with my mouth hanging open.

LUELLA. You said all that about Benny Schultz at first.

CAROLA. *(With a scream.)* Benny Schultz — my God! *(To EVAN.)* Do you know Benny Schultz.

EVAN. No, I don't.

CAROLA. *(Vehemently.)* Well, you'd better go down on you bended knees this very minute and pray with all your heart and soul that you never do.

EVAN. I think that would be a little excessive.

CAROLA. *(Standing over EVAN. Dramatically.)* Never again — never again as long as I live would I let that rat come within three blocks of me! What do you think he did?

EVAN. *(Shrinking back slightly.)* I haven't the faintest idea.

CAROLA. He directed me last year in a play called *The Goose Girl*. It was one of those little airy soufflé numbers that Sam Behrman adapts because somebody who can't understand French has seen it in Paris and loves it.

EVAN. I see.

CAROLA. Well, Mr Benny Schultz who burst on Broadway like an empty paper bag a few seasons ago, decides in that little tortured brain of his that he is going to teach me how to act, see?

EVAN. *(Nodding uncertainly.)* Yes.

CAROLA. Well — that's all right as a start. I let him have his head at rehearsals, because you can't make scenes in front of the company, but, oh boy, was I waiting! Well, it comes to the opening night in Washington — Washington, mark you! And I'm being sick as a dog because I always am on opening nights — when into my dressing room prances this synthetic Reinhardt and starts giving me notes after the first act — the *first* act, believe it or not! 'Listen Benny,' I said, 'You may have directed *Crazy Quilt, Mother's Day* and *The Wings of a Dove*, and you may have made Martha Cadman the actress she is, and Claudia Biltmore the actress she most certainly isn't, but you're not coming into my dressing room on an opening night and telling me that my tempo is too fast and that I struck a wrong note by taking my hat off at my first entrance. 'To begin with', I said, 'I had to take that god-awful hat off, which I never wanted to wear anyway — because the elastic band at the back was slipping, and if I hadn't, it would have shot up into the air and got a laugh in the middle of my scene with Edgar —' *(She pauses for breath.)* 'In the second place,' I said, 'if you had engaged a supporting company for me that could act and a leading man who had some idea of playing comedy and at least knew his lines, I wouldn't have to rush through like a fire-engine in order to carry a bunch of art-theatre hams who'd be miscast moving the scenery in summer stock. And in the third place, I should like to remind you that I was a star on Broadway when you were selling papers on the East Side, and I knew more about acting than you when I was five, playing the 'fit-ups' in *The Two Orphans*! And what's more, if you think I'm going to tear myself to shreds trying to get laughs in the supper scene in the pitch dark — well, you're out of your rotten little mind!' And I gave him a push like that — *(She pushes EVAN violently back on to the pillows.)* — and so help me God, if the son-of-a-bitch didn't fall backwards into the passage and crack his head against the wall and knock himself out!

BOB. Just plain clumsy.

CAROLA. *(Bending over the semi-recumbent EVAN. Vehemently.)* You've got to have light to play comedy and don't you forget it! *(She turns away.)* And all the highbrow directors in this world won't convince me otherwise.

LUELLA. For all that, I think Benny's pretty good.

CAROLA. He's alright with Shakespeare — I give you that. His *Macbeth* was fine — what you could see of it, but comedy — never! Look at the flop he had with *Some Take It Straight*.

LUELLA. *Some Take It Straight* was the worst play I ever sat through.

CAROLA. It needn't have been. I read the original script — they wanted me to do it with Will Farrow — than that rat got hold of it and bitched it entirely.

(LESTER and DON come back with two trays of drinks.)

LESTER. What's Carola yelling about?

LUELLA. Benny Schultz.

LESTER. I wouldn't trust him an inch — not an inch! Look what he did to *Macbeth*.

GLORIA. Open the window a bit, Bob — it's getting terribly fuggy in here.

BOB. *(Drawing the curtains and opening the window.)* Isn't this view peaceful and lovely, Mr Lorrimer? All that vast expanse of water and the lights glimmering in the distance —

LESTER. *(Handing round drinks.)* On a clear day you can see Elsa Maxwell.

DON. Would you like a drink, Mr Lorrimer?

EVAN. *(Fervently.)* More than anything in the world!

*(He takes one.
The door opens and IRENE MARLOW comes into the room. She is*

obviously fairly angry.)

    IRENE. Well, I'll be god-damned!
    LESTER. Irene, darling! —
    IRENE. Don't you 'darling' me, you ten-cent harlequin.
    LESTER. Why, whatever's the matter?
    IRENE. You know damned well what's the matter! You implore me to sing — you beseech me to sing — you say I'm divine and an angel and sheer heaven and that Mr Evan Thingummy-bob will never have a moment's peace or happiness until he hears me — then you all hide away in here and have a private party on your own and get stinking.
    CAROLA. We're not stinking, darling — and we're longing to hear you sing.
    IRENE. My eye!
    LESTER. We're coming now — this very minute.
    IRENE. *(Confronting EVAN menacingly.)* Do you or do you not want to hear me sing?
    EVAN. *(Starting to his feet.)* Very much indeed — I had no idea —
    IRENE. *(Grabbing him firmly by the arm.)* Come on then — what the hell are waiting for?

(She and EVAN go off, followed by the others laughing and talking as —
The lights fade.)

Scene 3

(The living room. About an hour later.

When the curtain rises, IRENE is just finishing a song. SUKI is at the piano. IRENE is standing in the cure of it, holding a chiffon handkerchief in her hand.

Near her, isolated from the rest, EVAN is seated on a stool.

Everyone else is sitting about the room. BRIGHT EYES and BONWIT are silently playing Bézique at their table downstage. Just above them CAROLA is in an armchair with LESTER perched on the arm of it. DON and BOB and GLORIA HOCKBRIDGE are sitting near the bar.

LOUISE is downstage right in an armchair with HUGHES HITCHCOCK sitting on the floor, leaning against her knees.

DWIGHT MACADOO and LUELLA ROSEN are on the sofa. Above the sofa DELIA and MARY-LOU BRANCATI have swivelled the chairs round from the backgammon table and are sitting facing the piano. LEONIE CRANE and SHIRLEY BENEDICT have put cushions on the floor and are sitting side by side on them just near BONWIT and BRIGHT EYES.

EVAN is looking fairly uncomfortable because he has had nothing to lean against and IRENE has already been singing for an hour.

IRENE sings "Never Again."* As she finishes overly dramatically, everyone applauds. During the applause LESTER jumps up and embraces IRENE.)

LESTER. Darling, that was wonderful! There's nobody like you — nobody in the world. Sing *Carbon Copy Lover*.

IRENE. Oh no, not that —
CAROLA. *Make Me Forget*.

---

*Sheet music for the song "Never Again" may be obtained from Warner Bros. Publications, Inc., 15800 N.W. 48th Avenue, Miami, FL 33014; Tel. 305-620-1500; Fax 305-621-1094.

LONG ISLAND SOUND

LOUISE. *My Heart's in a Covered Wagon.*

IRENE. I can't remember it — I haven't done it for ages.

DON. *Smoke Gets in Your Eyes.*

IRENE. *(Patiently.)* No dear —I really couldn't sing *Smoke Gets in Your Eyes.*

BOB. *(Sotto voce.)* Do *Smoke Gets in My Covered Wagon.*

MARY-LOU. *Why Did You Turn Away When I Said I Loved You?*

BOB. Her best friend wouldn't tell her.

GLORIA. *(Giggling.)* Shut up, dear.

IRENE. *(To EVAN.) You* choose — what would you like me to sing?

EVAN. *(Embarrassed.)* Anything — I don't mind a bit — I mean, it's all perfectly delightful.

IRENE. Please — I'd like to do something specially for you.

BOB. I know what's in his mind — I can read it like a book.

GLORIA. Shhh!

LESTER. Go on, honey — make a suggestion.

EVAN. I'm afraid I don't really know Miss Marlow's repertoire.

BOB. *(Sotto voce.)* He ought to have a rough idea of it after an hour and a quarter.

IRENE. *(Insistent.)* Come on — what's your favourite song? You must have one.

EVAN. *(Desperately.) Three Fishers Went Sailing.*

IRENE. I'm afraid I don't know that.

BOB. There *is* a God.

IRENE. I'm so awfully sorry.

EVAN. It doesn't matter a bit.

IRENE. I'll tell you what — I'll sing you a new number that Noël Coward wrote specially for me.

EVAN. Do — that would be charming.

IRENE. You won't mind if I go wrong in the lyric, will you?

EVAN. Not in the least.

IRENE. All right Suki — refrain — verse — refrain. B flat.
SUKI. That's too high for you –it means taking an F.
IRENE. A flat then.
SUKI. Right.

(SUKI plays an introduction and IRENE sings "Most of Every Day."
Her voice is deep and attractive and she sings with professional assurance.*
At the end of the song everyone applauds vociferously. There are ecstatic cries of 'Irene: Heaven! 'Enchanting!' 'Divine!' 'Out of this world' etc., etc.)

LESTER. *(When appreciation has faded a little.)* Do *Dearer Than a Dream.*
IRENE. No — I really can't do any more — I've sung far too much already.
BOB. Department of understatement.
LESTER. Just one more — be an angel — just one more —
CAROLA. Do an old one — something nostalgic.
IRENE. *(With amiable resignation.)* All right — this definitely is the last one, though.

(She leans across the piano and whispers to SUKI. He nods and she embarks on an extremely sentimental 'torch' song, "The Dream Is Over."*
While she is singing it, LOUISE lets her hand rest for a moment against HUGHSIE's face. He turns his head a little and kisses it.
DELIA looks round and LOUISE withdraws her hand with elaborate carelessness. DELIA shifts her chair a bit so that she can keep her eye on them.
When Irene has reached the middle of her nostalgic refrain, MRS

---

*Sheet music for the songs "Most of Every Day" and "The Dream Is Over" may be obtained from Warner Bros. Publications, Inc., 15800 N.W. 48th Avenue, Miami, FL 33014; Tel. 305-620-1500; Fax 305-621-1094.

BERNADINE GROUPER, LADY KETTERING and CHARLIE SCHOFIELD come in from the hall.

MRS GROUPER is a formidable old woman. She is heavily made-up and her hair is pastel blue and elaborately arranged. She is gaunt and there is something in her manner that suggests a predatory old bird. Her jewellery is impressive.

LADY KETTERING is a tall elderly Englishwoman. There is a certain rather ravaged distinction about her.

CHARLIE SCHOFIELD is a typical American playboy in the middle forties. He has that assured nonchalance that only far too much money can give. It is quite obvious from his appearance that he plays polo, tennis, golf, squash, bridge, backgammon, bézique, gin-rummy and poker. It is also inevitable that he has a speedboat, several cars and, possibly, a private plane.

This little group, upon observing with native astuteness that somebody is singing, tip-toe ostentatiously into the room.

LOUISE rises and hurries noiselessly across to them. She greets them in sibilant whispers.

EVAN who is seated immediately in their path, half gets up and, receiving a sharp look from IRENE, sits down again. LOUISE taps him on the shoulder. He looks up and she beckons him.

He gives an imploring look at IRENE and, getting up, inadvertently kicks over his highball glass which has been resting on the floor by his feet.

LESTER says 'Shhh!' IRENE continues her song with a baleful expression. EVAN joins LOUISE and the group of newcomers and is hissingly introduced to them.

IRENE, in a rage, finishes her song. Everyone applauds. As the applause is dying away she takes her bag off the piano and moves away.)

IRENE. Remind me to give a recital in Grand Central station sometime.

LOUISE. *(With great social poise.)* Irene — Mrs Grouper — you do know Irene Marlow, don't you?

MRS GROUPER. *(Extending a jewelled claw.)* How do you do?

IRENE. *(Sullenly.)* How do *you* do.

(Everyone in the room has risen to their feet. It is obvious that MRS GROUPER is the local equivalent of the Queen Mother.

LOUISE leads her reverently round the room introducing her to everybody. LADY KETTERING and CHARLIE SCHOFIELD follow after, greeting people as they go.

The conversation is general and indistinguishable.

JENKINS has emerged from the bar with a large tray of cocktails. LOUISE, while MRS GROUPER is momentarily occupied with the HUGHES HITCHCOCKS, darts over to BONWIT at the card table. There is one of those unaccountable lulls in the general noise.)

LOUISE. *(Hissing fiercely.)* Stop that damned game for a minute, you fool — it's Mrs GROUPER!

BONWIT. Christ!

(He gets up.)

BRIGIT. Saying two-fifty.

(The flood of conversation rises again. LOUISE takes BONWIT over to MRS GROUPER who greets him with graceful condescension. As the general hubbub begins to die down again the following lines are heard.)

JENKINS. *(To LADY KETTERING, who has sat down in the armchair vacated by CAROLA.)* 'Old fashioned' or dry martini, madam?

LADY KETTERING. Dry martini, please.
LEONIE. *(To SHIRLEY.)* I'll play you three games of ping-pong.
SHIRLEY. All right.

(Carrying their drinks, they go off on to the sun porch.
SUKI, MARY-LOU BRANCATI and the HUGHES HITCHCOCKS follow them.
THE HOCKBRIDGES, CAROLA, LESTER and IRENE vanish into the bar.
LOUISE, with EVAN and MRS GROUPER firmly in hand, finally ensconces them on the sofa.
DWIGHT MACADOO, CHARLIE SCHOFIELD and LADY KETTERING are left in a little group chatting.
BONWIT, his duties as a host discharged, goes back to BRIGHT EYES who is patiently waiting at the bézique table.

DWIGHT. *(To CHARLIE.)* Scrappy Bosworth's back from Palm Beach.

CHARLIE. He *can't* be.

DWIGHT. I saw him at The Colony.

CHARLIE. I thought he was going to Nassau on the Schreiber's yacht.

DWIGHT. That was called off. Fifi Schreiber had to have an operation.

LADY KETTERING. Why, for heaven's sake! What on earth for?

DWIGHT. Gall bladder.

LADY KETTERING. *(Sipping her martini.)* Poor beast.

LOUISE. *(To MRS GROUPER.)* It's so sweet of you to come. Evan has been so anxious to meet you. I said to him only this morning, 'Until you've met Mrs Grouper, you haven't seen America. Mrs Grouper *is* America.

MRS GROUPER. Nonsense, my dear — I'm just an old woman

and my life is over. *(To EVAN.)* How old do you think I am?

EVAN. I really couldn't say.

MRS GROUPER. Give a guess.

EVAN. *(Tentatively.)* Round about — sixty-four or five?

MRS GROUPER. *(Triumphantly.)* I shall be seventy-three next Tuesday.

EVAN. *(Politely.)* Really? I would never have thought it.

MRS GROUPER. I've done exactly what I wanted to ever since I can remember. That's the way to keep young.

EVAN. Yes — I expect it is.

LOUISE. *(Rising anxiously.)* Lady Kettering — do come over by the fire — Dwight — draw up a chair. Charlie — do come over here and join us.

(DWIGHT AND CHARLIE draw up a couple of chairs.
LADY KETTERING comes over and sits next to EVAN on the sofa.
CHARLIE and DWIGHT sit in the chairs.)

LOUISE. *(Calling.)* Bonwit — Bonwit —

BONWIT. *(Looking up.)* Yes, dear.

LOUISE. You might close the door to the bar — the noise is deafening.

BONWIT. Okay.

(He gets up and closes the door of the bar and returns to the table again.)

MRS GROUPER. *(Gripping EVAN's arm fiercely.)* I read your last book, Mr Lorrimer.

EVAN. *(Jumping.)* Oh — did you?

MRS GROUPER. And you may or may not know it, but you're my favourite man.

EVAN. *(Smiling nervously.)* How very kind of you to say so.

MRS GROUPER. *(Authoritatively.)* It's great literature. *(EVAN is about to deny this modestly but she holds up her hand and silences him.)* No — it's no use saying it isn't because *I know*. Henry James was a great friend of mine and I knew poor Edith Wharton too — intimately —we used to go to children's parties together.

EVAN. What fun.

MRS GROUPER. She was a sweet child and she grew up into a very, very wonderful woman. Did you ever know poor Millicent Crawshay?

EVAN. No — I'm afraid I didn't.

MRS GROUPER. That's a pity. She knew Edith Wharton too. Well, they're both dead now. Heigho.

LADY KETTERING. Do you like America?

EVAN. Immensely — of course I haven't seen very much of it — I've only just arrived.

LADY KETTERING. I've been here for three months. I'm going to Palm Beach. I think Palm Beach is bloody, don't you?

EVAN. I've never been there.

LADY KETERING. Well take my advice and don't go — it's filled with the most frightening people.

EVAN. I shan't be able to anyhow — I'm over to do a lecture tour.

LADY KETERING. How horrible! Whatever for?

EVAN. *(Slightly irritated.)* My publishers were very insistent that I should. Also I think it will be interesting to see something of America.

LADY KETTERING. You ought to go to Mexico — that's where you ought to go.

EVAN. I fear I shan't have time.

LADY KETTERING. That's the one thing you don't need in Mexico. Time doesn't exist. It's Paradise.

EVAN. *(Showing a little spirit.)* Why don't *you* go to Mexico instead of Palm Beach.

LADY KETTERING. I've promised to joint the Edlestons and go to Jamaica with them. Do you know the Edelstons?

EVAN. No.

LADY KETTERING. Well, take my advice and give them a wide berth. They're bloody.

MRS GROUPER. America is sadly changed, Mr Lorrimer. Of course, not having been here before, you won't know the difference, but I can assure you that what is happening to this country can only be described as tragic.

EVAN. In what way?

MRS GROUPER. In *every* way! We're doomed — completely and utterly lost.

LOUISE. Oh, come now Mrs Grouper — surely things aren't as bad as all that?

MRS GROUPER. *(Ignoring her.)* I remember years ago President Roosevelt saying to me — not this last New Deal man, I mean the other one — 'Laura,' he said, 'unless this country flings aside its swaddling clothes and grows up both socially and politically, we're as good as done for! We might just as well throw up the, 'What d'you call it!'

EVAN. Sponge.

MRS GROUPER. He said that to me personally and I shall never forget it until the day I die. He was a great man.

EVAN. So was the last President Roosevelt!

MRS GROUPER. *(Rising to her feet, trembling with rage.)* What did you say?

CHARLIE. Now then — don't get excited.

MRS GROUPER. *(Harshly.)* Excited! — I'm outraged!

EVAN. *(Firmly.)* I'm sure I fail to see why — I merely said that —

MRS GROUPER. *(Silencing him.)* Please — I really would prefer not to discuss the matter any further. *(She turns to LOUISE.)* Mrs Steinhauser — I've heard so much about your delightful house from my daughter. I should be pleased if you would show me some more of it.

LOUISE. *(Helplessly.)* I'm sure Mr Lorrimer — Evan — didn't mean —

MRS GROUPER. I fully realise that Mr Lorrimer is a stranger to our country, but as such I can only advise him to be a little more careful what he says. Come — Alice — Charlie — Mr Macadoo —

(Gripping LOUISE firmly by the arm she sweeps away.
LADY KETTERING and DWIGHT follow her. LOUISE shoots EVAN
an imploring look over her shoulder as they go.
CHARLIE laughs.)

EVAN. *(Angrily.)* Well, of all the damned nonsense — !

CHARLIE. Don't worry — you just happened to tread on her favourite corn, that's all.

EVAN. I'm not in the least worried — I'm extremely angry.

(The bar door opens and LESTER, the HOCKBRIDGES, CAROLA and IRENE come into the room. They join EVAN and CHARLIE by the fireplace.)

CAROLA. What's happened to the old Buddha?

LESTER. *(To EVAN.)* Honey — you look shattered — You need a little drinkie.

EVAN. I certainly do.

LESTER. *(Calling.)* Jenkins — bring a Scotch highball.

BOB. There seems to be a slight tension in the atmosphere. What happened?

EVAN. Nothing happened. I merely said that I thought Franklin D. Roosevelt was a great man — and I do.

BOB. That's no way to win friends and influence people on Long Island.

EVAN. I really fail to see why.

BOB. It's as bad as mentioning Mary Baker Eddy in the Vatican.

GLORIA. Mrs Grouper's stinking rich and an ardent Republican.

BOB. She was a big Wilkie girl in the last election and she'll be a big Taft girl in the next.

EVAN. I don't care what kind of a girl she is, she ought to have better manners.

LESTER. You mustn't let that old meat-axe upset you, honey. You ain't seen nothing yet — the woods are full of them.

EVAN. *(Still fuming.)* Louise said that until I met Mrs Grouper I hadn't *seen* America! She added that Mrs Grouper *was* America!

BOB. She didn't specify any particular part?

LESTER. *(Going into gales of laughter.)* The Painted Desert!

CHARLIE. Take it easy now, Lester — she's a great woman in her way.

EVAN. It doesn't happen to be a way I care for.

CHARLIE. Now see here, Mr Lorrimer —

LESTER. Now, let's all kiss and be friends — here's Jenkins with your drink, sweetheart. We'd better have some more all round. *(To Jenkins who has arrived with a Scotch highball for EVAN.)* Bring more wine, Jenkins, and order the dancing girls.

JENKINS. Yes, sir.

(JENKINS goes back to bar.)

CHARLIE. *(Rising.)* I'll have mine in the bar, I think.

(CHARLIE goes.)

LESTER. There goes the last of the Four Hundred!

EVAN. Who is he, anyhow?

BOB. Just the Playboy of the Western World.

CAROLA. Believe it or not that man was crazy about me once — years ago when I was playing *The Eighth Mrs Ives* — sweet God, I've never watched so much polo in my life.

(LEONIE and SHIRLEY come out of the sun porch followed by all the others. They are breathing heavily.)

LEONIE. Bring me a drink somebody — I'm whacked.

(She flings herself into an armchair.)

GLORIA. Who won?
LEONIE. Shirley — she beat the hell out of me.

(SHIRLEY sits on the floor with her head against LEONIE's knees.
MARY-LOU BRANCATI and LUELLA sit at the backgammon table and start to play.
SUKI goes over to the piano and begins to strum idly. An improvisation — use a recognizable song.
JENKINS comes out of the bar with a tray of drinks.
IRENE wanders over to the piano and hums whatever SUKI is playing.
CHARLIE comes out of the bar. The HUGHES HITCHCOCKS are obviously having an argument but it is impossible to hear what they say.
The noise becomes deafening.
EVAN sits miserably on the corner of the sofa clutching his drink.)

LEONIE. Enjoying your rest, Mr Lorrimer?
EVAN. *(Leaning forward.)* What?
LEONIE. *(Shouting.)* ENJOYING YOUR REST?
EVAN. *(Shouting back.)* IMMENSELY.

(At this moment LOUISE appears from the hall with MRS GROUPER, LADY KETTERING and DWIGHT.)

LOUISE. *(Clapping her hands gaily.)* Dinner, everybody! Bring your drinks in with you....

(The noise rises and the lights fade.)

Scene 4

(The living room. About two hours later.

When the curtain rises, EVAN is sitting by the fire gloomily turning the pages of Town and Country.

There is an atmosphere of unwonted peace in the room. BONWIT and BRIGHT EYES are still quietly playing bézique. They occasionally murmur to each other.

At a card table by the window MRS GROUPER, LUELLA, CHARLIE and LADY KETTERING are playing bridge. They also make a staccato remark every now and then but their game is too concentrated for such conversation.

DELIA HUGHES HITCHCOCK comes in from the sun porch. She is wearing what might be described as a 'set' expression. She is also a trifle unsteady on her feet and carries an empty highball glass.)

DELIA. I hate women who drink. They make me sick.

EVAN. It probably makes *them* sick, too.

DELIA. *(Puzzled.)* What does?

EVAN. Drink.

DELIA. Oh. *(Pause as she lets that irrefutable logic sink in.)* I hate women who do other things even more.

EVAN. What sort of things?

DELIA. *(With vehemence.)* Women who play cheap, rotten tricks — women who cheat.

EVAN. Yes — they can be very disagreeable.

DELIA. Have you known Louise long?

EVAN. No — not very long.

DELIA. *(Leaning towards him with a slight stagger.)* Well, be careful — that's all I have to say to you — just be careful.

EVAN. Wouldn't you like to sit down?

DELIA. *(Belligerently.)* Why should I?

EVAN. No particular reason — I merely though that you might find it more comfortable than standing up.

DELIA. What are you insinuating?

EVAN. I'm not insinuating anything.

DELIA. Oh, yes, you are — you can't fool me — I can always tell.

EVAN. I have no intention of fooling you.

DELIA. *Nobody* can fool me — although I know certain people who *think* they can.

EVAN. Well, if you won't sit down, I think I will – I'm rather tired.

(He does so.).

DELIA. *(Firmly.)* I want my husband — and I want to go home.

EVAN. Both very laudable desires.

DELIA. And you know where he is.

EVAN. No I don't.

DELIA. You do, too — You're holding out on me. I can always tell.

EVAN. *(With rising irritation.)* I assure you that I haven't the faintest idea where your husband is. I don't even know *who* he is.

DELIA. You were talking to him before lunch.

EVAN. I've been talking to hundreds of people all day. I've never talked to so many people in my life — and I don't want to talk to any more — so if you will forgive me, I'll go on reading my magazine.

DELIA. So typical of the shallow approach the men of today take to real life. I had hoped you might have been deeper, more sensitive. But I see I was wrong. You would rather read a magazine than deal with relationships. Go on, read your — magazine. I shall find my — *(She stumbles over the word she wants.)* — hub-sband myself.

(She weaves her way with unsteady dignity towards the door and exits, almost bumping into LESTER, who is coming in, carrying two empty glasses. He senses what has happened and laughs. This is something he's seen before.)

LESTER. I see it's your turn to play a scene with Madame Borgia. Poor you. Have you seen Don? He's supposed to be in charge of refills and he always takes the longest time when he's losing.

EVAN. *(Rather stiffly.)* No, I'm afraid not. I'll tell him you were looking for him, if I see him.

LESTER. We're playing our own genteel version of strip poker. Very modest. Nothing beyond our Sulka underwear. And a *lot* of fun. Does the idea appeal? Come and sit next to me — I'll teach you.

EVAN. *(Firmly.)* Even that supreme inducement will not tempt me, Lester. My mind is made up.

LESTER. *(Laughing hilariously.)* 'Supreme inducement'! You're divine — you really are — I'm nuts about you!

EVAN. Good.

LESTER. I'm just going to play one more hand and then we'll have a lovely long talk — we'll let our hair *right* down — but to the ground!

DON. *(Emerging from the bar carrying two highballs.)* Aren't you coming to play?

EVAN. No, thanks — I'm quite happy here.

DON. That's what I like to see — a guy that knows what he wants.

EVAN. It isn't a question of knowing what I want — it's a question of knowing what I most definitely *don't* want.

LESTER. *(Laughs admiringly.)* Isn't he heaven?

DON. You may not know it but you're coming to stay with me if you come to the Coast.

EVAN. It's very kind of you to suggest it.

DON. I insist. It's a very simple house, you know — none of that Spanish crap, but it's got a pool and a car and a skittle alley and I could let you have a car and an English valet.

LESTER. It's about as simple as Chartres Cathedral but you'll adore it — but seriously, you must go — it's an experience — if you know what I mean — and when I say *experience* — well .... *(He giggles.)*

DON. Don't pay any attention to what Les says — we happened to have a party when he was there — oh boy! —

EVAN. Oh boy, indeed.

DON. If you came you wouldn't be disturbed — you could do exactly what you liked.

EVAN. Thanks very much — I shall look forward to that.

LESTER. *(To DON.)* Come on, you great gorgeous thing — *(To EVAN.)* — Shan't be long, sweetheart.

(DON and LESTER go back on to the sun porch.
CHARLIE, who has become 'dummy' rises from the card table and comes over to EVAN.)

CHARLIE. *(Affably.)* I'm sorry I was short with you just now about old Mrs Grouper.

EVAN. Don't mention it.

CHARLIE. You see, we happen to have been friends for years.

EVAN. Congratulations.

CHARLIE. She's an extraordinary old girl, you know.

EVAN. So I gathered.

CHARLIE. So don't have it in for her, will you! I mean — she doesn't mean half she says and she's crazy about you anyhow — she's crazy about all writers as a matter of fact.

EVAN. That rather vitiates the compliment, doesn't it?

CHARLIE. So forget about the whole business, won't you?

EVAN. Utterly.

CHARLIE. I believe you know a great friend of mine.

EVAN. Do I — who?

CHARLIE. The Duke of Windsor.

EVAN. I met him a couple of times when he was Prince of Wales — but I couldn't really say that I knew him.

CHARLIE. He's a grand guy — absolutely genuine — I used to play polo with him a lot — Do you play polo?

EVAN. No — I don't ride well enough.

CHARLIE. It's a grand game. I used to play on Boots Leavenworth's team. You know Boots Leavenworth, of course?

EVAN. *(Lying.)* Of course — he's awfully nice.

CHARLIE. I suppose you don't know what's happened about him and Daphne?

EVAN. *(Lost.)* I — I — er — think things are much the same.

CHARLIE. You mean Rollo's still holding out?

EVAN. *(Firmly.)* When I left England — Rollo was still holding out.

CHARLIE. Some people are peculiar, aren't they? To tell you the truth I always thought him a bit of a bastard — outwardly amusing enough, you know — but shifty.

EVAN. Shifty's the word.

CHARLIE. As a matter of fact poor Tiger's the one I'm sorry for, aren't you?

EVAN. Desperately.

CHARLIE. Where is Tiger now?

EVAN. *(Racking his brains.)* Er — I don't know — Africa, I think.

CHARLIE. Good God! You don't mean to say he's thrown his hand in and left poor Iris to cope with everything?

EVAN. I suppose he must have.

CHARLIE. This is appalling! I must tell Alice Kettering — she'll be in a terrible state.
EVAN. *(Hurriedly.)* Please don't — it may only have been a rumour — you know how people gossip!
CHARLIE. I can hardly believe it — I won't tell her until after this rubber.
LADY KETTERING. Charlie —
CHARLIE. Coming.

(He goes back to the table.)

LADY KETTERING. I'm afraid we went down.
EVAN. *(Audibly.)* Oh God!

(IRENE comes out of the bar and weaves her way over to EVAN. She is obviously very drunk indeed. She sinks down on to the sofa beside him.)

IRENE. Baby's fried.
EVAN. I beg your pardon?
IRENE. Stinkalino.
EVAN. *(Laughing nervously.)* Oh yes, of course — Stinkalino.
IRENE. *(Defensively.)* Who said so?
EVAN. You did.
IRENE. Then I was dead right. *(She looks round unsteadily.)* Where is everybody?

(Her head lolls back.)

EVAN. *(Agitated.)* Look here — wouldn't you like me to order you some black coffee or something?
IRENE. *(Sitting up again.)* D'you know something? — I think you're the most attractive man I ever met in my whole life —

EVAN. Thank you very much — I'm most flattered.

IRENE. D'you like me a little, too?

EVAN. Of course I do.

IRENE. How much?

EVAN. A little.

IRENE. Funny, hey!

EVAN. I mean that I only known you a little — we met today for the first time.

IRENE. You were so sweet when I was singing — sitting there all hunched up and staring and staring at me with those great big eyes. Remember?

EVAN. *(Soothingly.)* Yes — yes — I remember distinctly.

IRENE. *(Nestling against him.)* You're sweet — I could go for you in a big way.

EVAN. *(Shrinking away.)* Well, please don't, there's a dear — somebody might see.

IRENE. You remind me of somebody I once loved very much indeed — he had sinus trouble.

EVAN. What a pity. Please sit up, Miss Marlow.

IRENE. *(Lying across him — drowsily.)* D'you know something about the British?

EVAN. Yes — a great deal.

IRENE. They're the most wonderful people in the whole world — their films are good, too.

EVAN. I'm very glad you think so.

IRENE. Let's go home now — just you and me.

EVAN. I'm afraid that's out of the question.

IRENE. That's what I love about the British — they're so formal.

(She closes her eyes.
EVAN looks round anxiously. The bridge party is breaking up.)

MRS GROUPER. *(To Charlie.)* Leave it to me. *(She marches*

firmly over to EVAN.) Mr Lorrimer.

EVAN. *(With as much dignity as he can manage with IRENE stretched across him.)* Yes, Mrs Grouper.

MRS GROUPER. I wish to apologise.

EVAN. Please don't — it's quite unnecessary.

MRS GROUPER. I snapped at you — don't deny it. I know I did.

EVAN. It doesn't matter in the least.

MRS GROUPER. I'm an old woman, Mr Lorrimer.

EVAN. Yes, I know — you told me. Please forgive me for not getting up but as you see I am unable to at the moment.

MRS GROUPER. That's the woman who was singing when we came in, isn't it?

EVAN. Yes, it is.

MRS GROUPER. What's the matter with her?

EVAN. I think she's a little — tired.

MRS GROUPER. Nonsense. She's drunk. Just like the poor Harriet Templeton — tight as a tic from morning till night. She was one of my greatest friends.

EVAN. Oh.

MRS GROUPER. I want you to prove that you have forgiven me, Mr Lorrimer.

EVAN. I assure you there is nothing whatever to forgive.

MRS GROUPER. Rubbish. I was perfectly insufferable and I am quite aware of it. I want you to come and stay with me next weekend. I will send a car in for you — where are you staying?

EVAN. The Plaza but —

MRS GROUPER. Then that's all arranged. You can be absolutely quiet and do whatever you like — there'll be nobody in the house except the Reardons, the Seligmans and dear old Maud Beamish.

EVAN. It's extremely kind of you but I'm afraid I can't possibly manage it — I shall be lecturing in Boston next weekend.

MRS GROUPER. Put it off.

EVAN. I can't put it off.

MRS GROUPER. Why not?

EVAN. That's the reason I'm here — to do a lecture tour.

MRS GROUPER. Absurd.

EVAN. It may seem absurd to you — but it happens to be the truth.

(LADY KETTERING followed by CHARLIE join the group.)

LADY KETTERING. What's all this about Tiger?

EVAN. *(Becoming rattled.)* All what?

LADY KETTERING. You told Charlie that he'd gone to Africa.

EVAN. Well, if he hasn't, he should have.

LADY KETTERING. When did you last see him?

EVAN. *(Beginning to lose control.)* I've never seen him in my life and I don't want to.

LADY KETTERING. The man's raving mad!

CHARLIE. You told me distinctly —

MRS GROUPER. Eleven-thirty next Saturday morning the car will be at The Plaza — that will get you down in a time for a cocktail before lunch. I'll get some people over.

EVAN. I've already explained, Mrs Grouper, that I can't possibly come next weekend — I shall be lecturing in Boston.

MRS GROUPER. Why?

EVAN. Because my publishers want me too.

MRS GROUPER. Who are they?

EVAN. Foley and Bloch.

MRS GROUPER. Bring them as well — can they play bridge?

EVAN. I don't know.

MRS GROUPER. Bring them anyhow — we'll fit them in somewhere. Come along Alice — Charlie — you come with me. Good night, Mr Lorrimer. It has been both an honour and a pleasure to meet so distinguished a writer as yourself. Until next weekend then — *a bientôt*!

(MRS GROUPER churns away into the hall followed by LADY KETTERING and CHARLIE SCHOFIELD.
LESTER, DWIGHT, LUELLA and DON come on from the sun porch.)

LESTER. *(Seeing IRENE lying across EVAN's lap, stops dead.)* Sweet God! Love in bloom!

LUELLA. *(Going over to IRENE.)* Snap out of it, dear. It's all right to be reasonably hospitable to visiting celebrities, but you don't have to lie on them.

(She drags IRENE off EVAN's lap and leans her against the sofa cushions.).

IRENE. Baby wants a drink.

LUELLA. Baby wants a nice pot of black coffee and an ice pack.

IRENE. You think I'm drunk, don't you?

LUELLA. That shameful thought had occurred to me.

IRENE. Well, that's where you're wrong — I'm not drunk — just over-excited.

LUELLA. Deal with her, Dwight, for God's sake.

DWIGHT. *(Hoisting IRENE off the sofa.)* Here, beautiful — just you come along with Dwightie.

IRENE. Don't want to come along with Dwightie — Dwightie's a louse.

DWIGHT. *(Firmly.)* Come along.

IRENE. Where to?

LESTER. I give you three guesses.

IRENE. *(Witheringly to EVAN as DWIGHT leads her away.)* *Three Fishers Went Sailing*!

(DWIGHT and IRENE disappear into the hall.)

LESTER. *(Sitting on the sofa.)* She's an angel, Irene — but she certainly does get stinking — which reminds me — *(He claps his hands and calls.)* Jenkins — drinks for all the world *et sa femme.*

EVAN. Not for me. I'm going to bed.

LESTER. You must be mad! The party's only just beginning.

EVAN. *(Feelingly.)* God forbid!

LESTER. What's the matter honey? Aren't you feeling well?

EVAN. *(Irascibly.)* I'm feeling perfectly well but I wish to go to bed.

LESTER. All right, sweetheart — just you go to bed then and we'll all bring a little nightcap to you.

EVAN. I don't want a little nightcap.

LUELLA. *(Persuasively.)* Don't go quite yet, Mr Lorrimer — let's all just have one little quiet drink here by the fire — I haven't had a chance to talk to you all day and I had been so looking forward to meeting you.

EVAN. Really — if you don't mind I —

LESTER. Please, honey — you're among friends — you know we're all crazy about you —

DON. Come on — be a sport.

EVAN. I'm not a sport and I never was.

LUELLA. *(Sitting on his other side and slipping her arm through his.)* Please —

EVAN. *(With none too good a grace.)* Very well — if you insist.

(CAROLA and the HOCKBRIDGES come out from the sun porch. They are arguing heatedly.)

CAROLA. *(Not exactly drunk, but high.)* Well, if she's so wonderful, why not let *her* play my part? I can easily do the O'Neill play. The Guild has been holding it for me for ages.

BOB. Nobody can easily do an O'Neill play.

CAROLA. There's no sense in arguing. But I tell you here and now that if that saucer-eyed dumbcluck plays Anna I just won't open and that's that.

BOB. That's old-school stuff, Carola. You ought to know better than that.

GLORIA. Carola's quite right — there's no sense in arguing — let's discuss the whole business tomorrow.

CAROLA. Oh no, we won't, we'll settle it right now.

BOB. You're just being silly.

CAROLA. *(More incensed than ever.)* Silly! *(She turns to EVAN.)* Mr Lorrimer — as a writer — I appeal to you.

EVAN. I'm afraid I don't know what you're talking about.

CAROLA. *(Enraged.)* We're talking about Bob's play — that's what we're talking about. The play he wrote specially for me. The play he called me up twice a day for two months about wailing and screaming that if I didn't do it he'd never write another and that I was the only actress in the world who could possibly do it and —

BOB. For God's sake pipe down, Carola — this has nothing to do with Mr Lorrimer.

CAROLA. *(Ignoring him.)* Then, after we've been rehearsing two weeks I walks Miss Dulcie Laval, who's been flown out specially from the coast to play a part that could be played perfectly well by any competent Broadway actress for a hundred dollars a week. Not only that but she's to have feature billing and two scenes written in for her —

BOB. That's not true.

CAROLA. Don't lie to me — you know damn well it's true — and if you think I'm going to work like a lumberjack all through the first act to build up an entrance for that double-breasted MGM rocking-horse — you've got another guess coming.

LESTER. *(Laughing heartily.)* You're divine, Carola — you really are.

CAROLA. It's no laughing matter. I'm here to tell you once and for all that, if she plays the part I don't open, and that's all there is to it. Why, good God, she can't even act! All she does is stand about with her great big mouth pursed up as though she'd got a gooseberry in it.

DON. She certainly can't act — she was in a picture with me once and I know — but she has got sex appeal? Oh boy!...

CAROLA. *(Angrier than ever.)* Sex appeal! And what am I supposed to be in the play? A frustrated New England spinster?

BOB. You're definitely behaving like one.

GLORIA. *(Anxiously.)* Bob!

CAROLA. *(With deadly quiet.)* How *dare* you!

LESTER. Calm down, darling — Bob didn't mean it.

BOB. You bet your life I meant it. *(To CAROLA.)* Listen, Carola — I don't care how big a star you are. It's nothing to do with you who else is engaged in the cast. You have your name over the title and ten per cent of the gross and your job is to learn your words and say them properly. Neither of which you've done to date!

CAROLA. *(Breathing heavily.)* You rat! What can I throw at you!

BOB. Just my lines, dear.

*(He stalks off into the bar.
CAROLA flings herself sobbing into a chair.
GLORIA tries to comfort her.
JENKINS appears with a tray of drinks.)*

LESTER. Thank God! I can see lights — I can hear voices — we're SAVED!

CAROLA. *(Sobbing.)* Leave me alone — go away and leave me alone.

GLORIA. Don't pay any attention to Bob, darling — you know he gets like that when he's had a few drinks —

CAROLA. *(Mumbling.)* I don't care how many drinks he's had — he insulted me —

LESTER. *(Forcing a highball into her hand.)* Here, puss — have a little drink yourself — and you'll feel — but wonderful! *(At this moment angry voices are heard in the hall. LOUISE comes in hurriedly and comes over to the fireplace.)* Louise! — I haven't seen you since Good Friday — where have you been?

LOUISE. *(Obviously in a state of high nervous tension.)* I've been with Evan — up until a few moments ago — haven't I, Evan?

EVAN. *(Startled.)* What?

LOUISE. I had to go and see Mrs Grouper into her car — but until then I was with you, wasn't I? *(Imploringly.)* Wasn't I?

EVAN. *(Realising the situation.)* Yes, yes — of course you were — we were having a little chat — *(He looks round at the unbelieving faces.)* — about Robert Louis Stevenson.

DON. He once wrote a picture for me.

(DELIA comes in from the hall, followed miserably by HUGHSIE. She comes straight over to LOUISE.)

DELIA. Snake! Double-faced, rotten snake!

(DELIA slaps LOUISE's face hard.
Everyone jumps to their feet.
HUGHSIE makes a dive for DELIA and grabs her arm.)

HUGHSIE. Delia! For God's sake — don't be such a fool!

DELIA. I'm not such a fool as you think — as you *both* think — let go of me.

LOUISE. *(Trembling violently.)* Please leave my house.

DELIA. *(Loudly.)* You bet I'll leave your house — and what's more, I'm taking my husband with me — and you can put that in your pipe and smoke it.

HUGHSIE. Behave yourself! What do you mean by making a disgusting scene like this about nothing!

DELIA. Nothing? Do you suppose I don't know? Do you

suppose I haven't known, all along?

LOUISE. *(Rallying.)* Please take her home, Hughsie — she's drunk.

BRIGHT. *(To BONWIT.)* We'd better stop — something's happening.

BONWIT. *(Rising.)* Okay — remember it's your draw.

(He comes over, followed by BRIGHT EYES.)

DELIA. Drunk, am I?

LOUISE. Yes — as usual.

DELIA. *(Struggling.)* Let me get at her!

BRIGHT. For heaven's sake, control yourself, Delia — they'll hear you in Port Washington.

LOUISE. That would be no surprise to them. They've heard her all over Long Island at one time or another.

(LEONIE, SUKI, MARY-LOU and SHIRLEY come out of the sun porch.
BOB comes out of the bar.)

BONWIT. Delia —

DELIA. *(Breaking away from HUGHSIE.)* There's something about your wife that you don't know, Bonwit — something that you damn well ought to know.

HUGHSIE. Delia! SHUT UP!

DELIA. And if you weren't such a great silly ape you'd have known for yourself.

LOUISE. *(Wailing.)* Take her away — take her away —

DELIA. *(Breathing heavily.)* Don't anybody dare to touch me —

LESTER. This is fantastic — it really is — fantastic!

LOUISE. Leave my house this instant!

DELIA. I'll leave your house when I'm good and ready —

LOUISE. *(Losing all control.)* We'll see about that!

(LOUISE rushes at DELIA and shakes her like a terrier with a rat.
EVAN, being nearest, makes an attempt to pull her away but she gives him a violent push and he falls backwards over an occasional table, bringing everything on it crashing to the ground.
DELIA wriggles free from LOUISE, slaps her again and grabs her hair.
Everyone is talking at once. The noise is indescribable.
The lights fade.)

Scene 5

(The guest room. An hour or so later.
When the curtain rises, the room is in darkness. After a moment or two EVAN comes in wearily. He switches on the light and closes the door with a sigh of relief. He doesn't at first notice that IRENE is lying flat on her back on his bed. He finally sees her and stands transfixed with horror. Then he goes over and, taking her by the shoulder, shakes her violently.)

EVAN. Wake up.
IRENE. *(Grunting.)* G'way.
EVAN. Really, this is too much!

(He shakes her again.)

IRENE. *(Muttering.)* Leave me alone.
EVAN. Damn and blast the woman! *(he bends down and speaks loudly and clearly in her ear.)* Will you please wake up and go away — I want to go to bed.

IRENE. *(Opening an eye and looking at him.)* Why, it's you!

EVAN. Of course, it's me — this is my room.

IRENE. It's Fate! That's what it is — the hand of Fate.

EVAN. It isn't anything of the sort. Will you please get up and go away — I want to go to bed.

IRENE. You men are all alike — beasts!

(She giggles and closes her eyes again.)

EVAN. Please don't go to sleep again.

IRENE. *(Complacently.)* Only one thought in your minds.

EVAN. You misunderstand me, Miss Marlow. I don't want to go to bed *with* you, I want to go to bed *without* you.

IRENE. *(Happily and drowsily.)* That's what *you* say.

EVAN. For God's sake get up and don't be so idiotic. *(He shakes her.)* Miss Marlow — *(Shakes her again.)* — Miss Marlow!

(But it's no use, her head falls back and she is fast asleep. He looks round helplessly then, with a great effort, tries to lift her in his arms. She is very heavy and he staggers and drops her down on the bed again. His arms being round her, he falls with her. The door opens and DON comes in.)

DON. *(Obviously drunk.)* Lester — Les, where are you? — *(He sees EVAN and IRENE.)* Oh boy, oh boy, oh boy, oh boy, oh boy!!

EVAN. Don't be so silly! Help me.

DON. Help you what?

EVAN. Help me get her out, of course.

DON. What do you want to get her out for?

EVAN. Stay here a minute. *(He runs out into the bathroom. DON looks blearily after him. After a moment he returns with a wet sponge.)* This ought to do it.

DON. Do what?

EVAN. *(Almost shouting.)* Wake her up!
DON. Oh.

(EVAN places the wet sponge firmly on IRENE's face. She gives a cry and sits up.)

IRENE. *(Angrily.)* Who the hell did that?
EVAN. I did.
IRENE. Why you — you Communist!
EVAN. Will you please go away?
IRENE. I'm all wet.
EVAN. Serves you right!
IRENE. *(Suddenly seeing DON.)* What are you doing here?
DON. *(Hazily.)* I don't know — I'm looking for Les.
IRENE. *(Looking from one to the other and rising from the bed with dignity.)* I see. *(She walks grandly to the door.)* Pardon me for intruding!

(She sweeps out and slams the door after her.)

EVAN. What the devil did she mean by that?
DON. She's crazy. Everybody's crazy.
EVAN. *(Recovering his social poise.)* Well, good night — it's been so delightful meeting you.
DON. You know, I like you, pal.
EVAN. Thanks very much. I like you too.
DON. *(Penetratingly.)* Do you — do you really?
EVAN. *(Testily.)* Of course I do — but if you'll forgive me I —
DON. I like you better than any Englishman I've ever met. Most Englishman are high hat — you know — kind of snooty. But you're not high hat at all. You're a good sport.
EVAN. I'm sure it's very nice of you to say so but —
DON. You're not sore at me, are you?

EVAN. Not in the least.

DON. I wouldn't like you to be sore at me. It isn't often I get a chance to talk to anyone intelligent — not that you're only just intelligent, you're brilliant, otherwise you wouldn't be able to write all those goddamned books, would you?

EVAN. Look here —

DON. *(Aggressively.)* Now, don't argue! Of course you're brilliant and you know you are, don't you?

EVAN. Well — I wouldn't exactly say —

DON. *(Fondly.)* Of course you know — everybody knows when they're brilliant. They'd be damned fools if they didn't — look at the way you wisecrack Lester? If that isn't brilliant, I'd like to know what is. I'm just a simple sort of guy myself without any brains at all. I've got looks, I grant you that, otherwise I shouldn't be where I am today, should I? — but no brains — not a one. Why, the idea of sitting down and writing a letter drives me crazy, let alone a book. *(He goes despondently over to the window, draws the curtain and looks out for a moment.)* Sometimes when I see something beautiful like that — *(He indicates the view.)* — or when I run across someone really brilliant, like you — I feel low — honest to God, I do.

EVAN. *(Patiently.)* Why should you?

DON. Because I'm such a damn fool, of course. I couldn't write down what that looks like to me — not if you paid me a million dollars I couldn't. I couldn't paint it either. I couldn't even talk about it. What do I get out of life — I ask you?

EVAN. I don't know.

DON. *(Contemptuously.)* Money? Yes. I make a lot of dough and so what! Happiness? No. I'm one of the unhappiest sons-of-bitches in the whole world.

(He bursts into tears.)

    EVAN. Please don't cry — there's nothing to cry about.

DON. It just gets me down, that's all. It gets me down.

EVAN. *(Soothingly.)* Now, why don't you go away and find yourself another little drink?

DON. Swell — come on.

(He takes EVAN's arm.)

EVAN. No, I don't want one.

DON. Come on — be a sport.

EVAN. I can't — *(An inspiration strikes him.)* I've got a date.

DON. A date?

EVAN. *(Recklessly.)* Yes — with a blonde — a great big gorgeous blonde!

DON. *(Impressed.)* No kidding! You British sure do work fast.

EVAN. We muddle through.

(He pushes DON gently towards the door.).

DON. Well — I'll be shoving off now. So long, pal.

EVAN. So long — and cheer up.

DON. Okay, pal — okay.

(DON goes out.

EVAN closes the door after him and sinks on to the bed for a moment with his head between his hands. Then, with an effort, he begins to undress. He takes his shoes off, then his coat which he hangs neatly over the back of a chair. He is just taking his tie off when he hears someone coming.

Quick as a flash he jumps into bed, draws the covers up to his chin and switches off the light.

There is a tap on the door, then it opens gently and LESTER tiptoes into the room. He switches on the light. He is wearing his dressing-gown and pyjamas and carrying an extra pillow.

EVAN pretends to be asleep.)

LESTER. Honey! *(EVAN gives a slight snore. LESTER shakes him gently.)* Honey, I didn't mean to disturb you but I've got to sleep in here — in the other bed.

EVAN. *(Waking up rather too quickly.)* What? — Why?

LESTER. I'll be quiet as a mouse — I've got to get up early in the morning but I'll dress in the bathroom and you won't hear a sound.

EVAN. Why can't you sleep in your own room?

LESTER. Bonwit's in there — Louise is still having hysterics and Luella is going to stay with her — all the other rooms are full. I promise I won't disturb you.

EVAN. I don't wish to appear ungracious but I really do loathe sharing a room with anybody. I'm a very light sleeper. Isn't there really anywhere else you can go?

LESTER. Not so much as a closet — the row's still going on — everybody's screaming — I was enjoying it up to a point but now it's gone too far — I'm exhausted.

EVAN. So am I.

LESTER. I could murder Louise — I really could.

EVAN. So could I.

LESTER. *(Arranging his bed.)* I wish now I'd never sent her to Dr. Gottlieb — she isn't nearly as inhibited as I thought.

EVAN. Personally, I never wish to set eyes on her again.

LESTER. It's so unfortunate that all that should have happened just when we were having such a wonderful time.

EVAN. You may have been having a wonderful time — I most certainly wasn't. I've never spent such a hideous day in my life.

LESTER. Long Island isn't all like this, you know.

EVAN. I should bloody well hope not.

LESTER. In the old days before the war it was much more exclusive — I mean, people didn't have quite such *mixed* parties.

EVAN. You mean they all got drunk in front of each other instead of getting drunk in front of strangers.

LESTER. *(Giggling.)* I adore you when you say witty things like that.

EVAN. I am feeling far from adorable.

LESTER. But really and truly this isn't typical — I swear it isn't.

EVAN. Good.

LESTER. In the old days when one used to stay with the Brophys or the Van Zimmermans it was perfectly enchanting — I suppose you never knew old Chloe Van Zimmerman.

EVAN. *(With steel in his voice.)* No, Lester, I never did. Nor did I know Sue Brophy or Jane Trumpet or Clara Summerford or Wee Wee Macpherson or even old Maud Beamish and I'm here to tell you, honey boy, that if by any horrid chance I happen to meet any one of them on my lecture tour, I shall spit in their eye and blind them!

LESTER. Why, Evan — !

EVAN. *(Mowing him down.)* And what's more — sweetheart — if you mention any more names to me that I neither know nor wish to know — if you say 'who shall be nameless,' 'if you know what I mean' or 'honey' — to me in any circumstances whatever — in fact if you so much as open your goddamned trap — as God is my judge, I'll tear the liver and the lights out of you and bash your silly head to a pulp!

LESTER. *(Astounded.)* Evan!

EVAN. *(Sternly.)* Not one more word, now. Turn out the lights. Get into bed, go to sleep and SHUT UP!

(LESTER, completely crushed, tiptoes over the window, opens it, creeps back to the bed, slips silently into it and switches off the light.

The moonlight shining through the window illuminates the two motionless figures.

After a moment or two EVAN very quietly slips out of his bed and proceeds, with the greatest caution, to continue his undressing.

He is about to take his shirt off when LESTER begins to snore. He stops. LESTER snores louder.

EVAN stands staring at him in anguished perplexity. Then a thought strikes him. He tiptoes over to the bed table and, finding the little box of ear plugs, stuffs them into his ears. He then goes and sits on the chaise-lounge and listens.

LESTER continues to snore. The ear plugs are obviously inadequate to cope with the situation so EVAN takes them out and pitches them angrily into a corner of the room. The, after further thought, he makes his great decision.

Quickly and silently he put on his shoes and his coat and his tie. He glances at his wrist-watch which has a luminous dial — picks up his overcoat and hat which have fallen down behind the chaise-lounge, puts them both on, feels in the overcoat pocket for a scarf which he ties round his neck and, going softly to the door, opens it.

He is greeted by the sound of VOICES in the passage. There are several voices but LOUISE's is easily distinguishable. She is screaming, 'Never, never again.'

EVAN closes the door again hurriedly and stands there trapped and breathing heavily.

LESTER continues to snore

EVAN, with a muttered curse, goes over to the window and leans out. Then, obviously bracing himself for the effort, he climbs on to the sill and lets himself carefully over the edge.

There is a moment's pause and then a loud cry and a crash of breaking glass.

LESTER stops snoring, turns over in his sleep and hunches himself up under the covers.

LESTER. *(Dreamily.)* Who shall be nameless!

CURTAIN

COSTUMES AND PROPERTIES

Except where specifically stated in the text, costumes are directorial choice. There is room for directorial discretion with props but the following would seem to be minimal requirements.

THE GUEST ROOM
Twin beds
Bedside table
Cigarette box and lighter
Table lamp
Wall mirror
Pile of books
Chaise longue
Armchair
Ear plugs
Sponge
Water carafe and two glasses

THE LIVING ROOM
Baby grand piano and stool
Sofa and coffee table
At least two occasional or card tables with two upright chairs at each
Several armchairs which can be moved to form different groupings
Several cigarette boxes and table lighters
Cards for bézique
Backgammon set
Magazines
Jenkin's drinks tray
Endless glasses for the nonstop drinks.
(In the TACT production, individual drinks were served!)

SOUND EFFECTS

Fog horn
Cars arriving and departing

ABOUT THE SET

The guest room takes up the top left quarter of the stage.

When the action is set there, the lighting keeps the rest of the set in darkness. When the action takes place in the living room, the lights come up on the whole set and the guest room is hidden behind a moveable screen or drop.

The hall area—supposedly leading to the front door, the stairs and the rest of the house—has double doors into the living room. When they are closed during the guest room scenes, that area can be assumed to be the bathroom leading into the guest room and beyond it to Lester's room and the corridor. Evan goes into it at various times and others enter through it.

In the living room, there is a door (Left) which supposedly leads into the bar.

Opposite there is a set of French windows that lead to the sun porch.

The room has a number of small card tables and an assortment of chairs—both armchairs and straight-back chairs—that can be rearranged in different configurations as needed. The two-person bézique table is occupied virtually throughout by Bright Eyes and Bonwit. Another table with four chairs is used for backgammon and later for bridge.

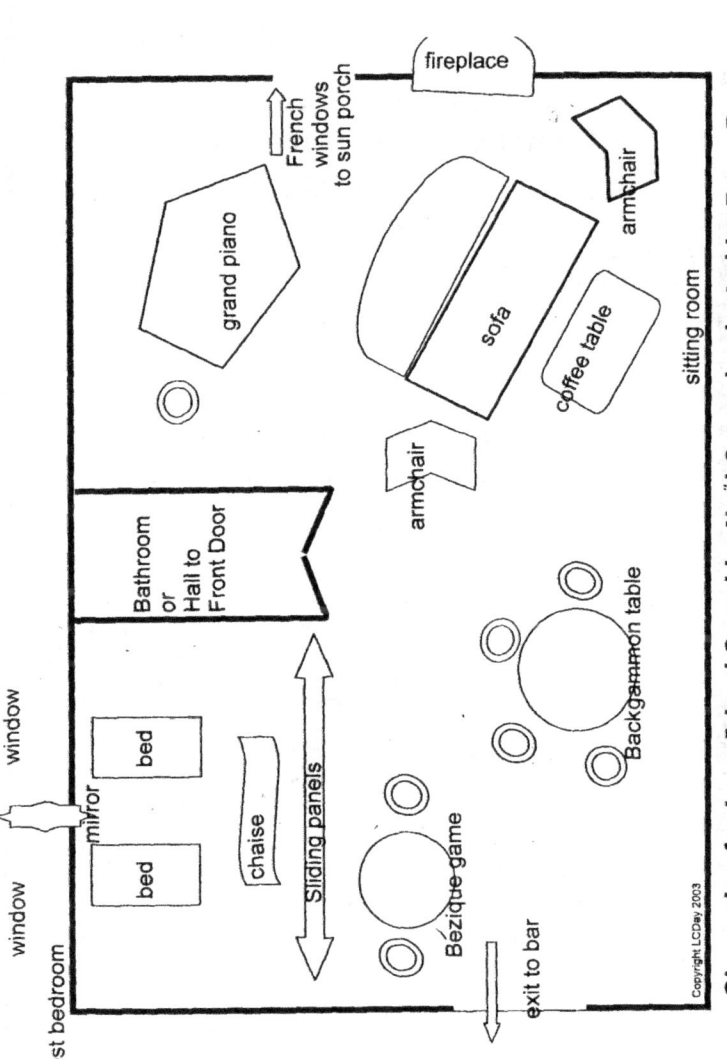

NOW AVAILABLE FROM SAMUEL FRENCH

Explosions and more ...
A Complete Sound Effects Library

From plains and trains to household sounds, wind, rain and thunder, background noises from carnivals to cocktail parties, shots and explosions of all kinds, here is a CD library with over 500 sound effects for professional sounding productions.

Sound effects package (8 CDs): $195.00 (#79991).

*PRS (Play Rehearsal Scheduler)
A production book in your computer

PRS is a time-saving tool that simplifies organizing and managing both large and small shows. It provides directors, stage managers and producers with outlines for rehearsal schedules; cast requirements per scene; set and crew movements; costume, prop and vendor tracking; soundtrack and music cues; cast and crew contract data; play breakdowns with notes to use during performances; management of scene diagrams: cast picture files and more.

"Tremendously useful.... This powerful, customized data-base program ... will solve many production needs."—*Stage Directions*

"I don't know how I produced and directed plays in the past without PRS!!"—*Russell Weisenbacher, English/Drama Teacher, N. Massapequa, NY*

"I love the software."— *Kris Adams, Limestone Community High School, Barontonville, IL*

CD with on-screen help manual: $89.00 (#55234)
Additional printed manual: $15.00 (#55235)